OF RICE AND MEN

OF RICE AND MEN

FROM BATAAN TO V-J DAY

A SURVIVOR'S STORY

BY

BOB REYNOLDS

Mindanao Books
2019

Of Rice and Men: From Bataan to V-J Day, a Survivor's Story by Bob Reynolds. First published in 1947.

Revised edition published by Mindanao Books, 2019.

FIRST PRINTING 2019.

ISBN: 9781099931000.

Contents

1 - The Beginning of the End 7
2 - War in the Philippines 12
3 - The Battle of Bataan 18
4 - The Death March 38
5 – Back to Bataan 43
6 - Cabanatuan 62
7 - Lipa, Batangas 67
8 - Bilibid Prison 71
9 - Return to Cabanatuan 80
10 - En Route to Dai Nippon 85
11 - The Land of the Rising Sun 89
12 - The Setting of the Sun 104
13 - The End 108

1 - THE BEGINNING OF THE END

"Because one of your number has escaped, five men must be punished. As I call your names, you will step forward to be executed."

BY THE GRACE OF GOD, it was another narrow escape from death, but let me relate the circumstances...

In the eight months prior to Pearl, many of the nation's youth responded to the call to colors in America's fast-growing armed forces. In March of 1941, I saw fit to disrupt my educational career as a sophomore in college in compliance with Uncle Sam's behest, "I WANT YOU!"

After three months of basic ground training at Jefferson Barracks in St. Louis, I was sent to an Air Corps Technical School at Denver, Colorado. There, over a four-month comprehensive course, I studied various phases of Air Corps administration and communications and upon graduation was assigned to the ill-fated Thirty-fourth Pursuit Squadron at Hamilton Field, California.

By this time, I had seven months of service but as yet hadn't seen any practical work; consequently, I was thrilled at the prospect of having been assigned to a tactical pursuit squadron. If it was action and adventure I was anticipating, I had certainly been delegated to the right organization, for upon reporting to my commanding officer I learned that the squadron was assigned under sealed orders to depart for foreign service within two weeks.

I had time to become acquainted with the nature of my work and most of the pilots and men in the organization when we embarked on board the *S.S. President Coolidge* for an undisclosed port. Our mailing address was:

"Plum, c/o Postmaster, San Francisco, California."

The date was November 1, 1941. The aforementioned *S.S. President Coolidge* was the flagship of the President Lines and had not been converted from her luxury liner status into a troop transport.[1]

We enjoyed the comforts of first-class world travelers en route to the Orient because all the civilian employees of the line had been hired under yearly contract and were a part of the ship when the government requisitioned her. The ship's orchestra played in the dining salon at meal-time and gymnastics, and swimming instructors were on hand to supervise our recreation.

As we sailed from the San Francisco harbor, I stood on deck watching the Golden Gate Bridge fade from view, and wondering just how long it would be before I would see it again. Often during the intervening years, I wondered too.

Three hours out from the Golden Gate, we were told that our first stop would be Honolulu. From the ship's crew, we learned that stops were scheduled at Honolulu, Guam, Manila and Hong Kong before returning to an American West Coast port with American refugees from the Orient. We were certain to disembark at one of these ports, but which one would it be?

On the morning of the fifth day at sea, we sighted Diamond Head, the mariner's guide to Honolulu's harbor.[2] Several hours later, we docked alongside the Aloha Tower and were welcomed in the traditional Hawaiian manner by a string orchestra and a company of lascivious hula dancers who boarded the ship. Then all hands went ashore to see and taste the magic of Hawaii.

Necklaced with leis, two buddies and I strolled down Honolulu's famed Avenue of Palms to be greeted subtly by a sign, "DO NOT URINATE ON STREET!"

---

[1] A few months later, on January 12, 1942, the *Coolidge* hit two mines in the Philippines' Espiritu Santo harbor and was forced to run aground. Captain Elwood Joseph Euart's decision to try and beach his ship saved the lives of five thousand men, but he was court-martialed for the loss of the vessel. Today, the wreckage of the *Coolidge*, in the accessible shallow waters of Vanuatu, is one of the world's most popular dive sites.

[2] The volcanic crater landmark Diamond Head is known to the locals as Lēʻahi, and in the age of sail was the "mariner's guide" to espy the harbor at Honolulu.

After a three-dollar plate dinner of burned steak at one of the city's better eating places, we hired a cab to Waikiki Beach where we visited the Hotel Royal Hawaiian and cut our feet on the coral of the beach.

Eight hours later, poorer but wiser men, we once more boarded the ship, which slid gently out of the harbor to the strains of "Aloha" and "Beautiful Hawaii." Two hours out of Pearl Harbor, we were joined by our naval escort, the cruiser Louisville, that was to be our constant companion throughout the remainder of the voyage.

War was impending even then, as evidenced by our cruiser escort. For additional precaution, the ship was completely blacked out at night. The daily news bulletin was filled with data regarding diplomatic negotiations with Japan. At a point twelve days out of Hawaii, an unidentified vessel which appeared on the horizon refused to acknowledge the blinker signals dispatched from the cruiser. In less than a minute, our escort had launched two airplanes, and made a ninety-degree turn, heading full speed toward the unidentified craft. All must have proven well, however, as half an hour later she was running again in her usual position.

On November 20, 1941, we disembarked at Manila, and it was then that I was introduced to the smell of the Orient. To describe this odor is difficult but if one can conceive a combination of the aromas of garlic, perfume, sweating horses, and marijuana, he has a general idea. From the pier, we were taken to Nichols Field, where the squadron uncrated its equipment shipped from the California base and proceeded to set up flight operations. After five days at Nichols Field, we received orders from USAFFE[3] to change stations.

Given only rough road maps and compass directions, we spent most of the night reaching our destination, a newly-built airstrip near Del Carmen, Pampanga, about one hundred kilometers north of Manila. Upon arrival at Del Carmen, we were pleased to find the field inhabited by a company of aviation

---

[3] United States Armed Forces in the Far East.

engineers who had leveled the five-mile runway and were now in the process of surfacing the field.

Since we arrived just before dawn, the engineering unit's invitation to breakfast with them was indeed welcome. By noon of that day, everything was in order. Tents were pitched, field equipment was set up and everything was in readiness for our ships, which were to be flown up that afternoon from Manila.

For the following week things progressed in routine. We found a delightful swimming hole in a river that ran parallel with the field and drove trucks to the spot every evening.

While we were busy exploring our new surroundings, the engineers continued their task of surfacing the runways with molasses. This operation seemed very stupid to me until I learned that molasses encouraged the growth of a certain hearty-rooted tropical grass which would make an excellent surface for our planes' landing wheels.

At the end of that first week in Del Carmen we received orders once more from our headquarters; this time to dig air raid shelters and revetments for our planes. With this message came an order for our commanding officer to report to nearby Clark Field at once. When the C.O. returned that evening, we had completed digging shelters to accommodate our two hundred and sixteen men. Even before the propeller of his plane stopped turning, he had summoned every man in the squadron.

With grave expression he informed us that war was practically upon us. G-2[4] had information of nine hundred heavy Japanese bombers, based on the southern tip of Formosa,[5] a bare three hundred miles from Luzon[6]; theirs could be but one objective: The Philippines!

For thirty seconds complete silence reigned; then the calm authoritative voice of our commanding officer reminded us that we had been thoroughly trained for this eventuality and

---

[4] Military Intelligence.

[5] Taiwan.

[6] Luzon is the main island of the Philippines, home to Manila; the other two major islands are Visayas and Mindanao.

that he expected us to carry on our work in the same efficient manner we had thus far displayed.

We listened to this speech on the evening of December 7, 1941. In America it was December 6, because of the International Dateline. The following morning our radio section reported that Pearl Harbor had been bombed by Japanese carrier-based planes.

2 - WAR IN THE PHILIPPINES

ALL OF THAT DAY WE RECEIVED last-minute radio instructions from Air Force Headquarters; orders for offense and defense, instructions for the issuance of gas masks and combat equipment, and directives to arm our pursuit planes with ammunition and wing bombs.

In my department, our work became quite complicated. Daily reports had assumed a nature of vital importance, both to our headquarters and the enemy. Each morning a radio report in code was sent to USAFFE giving them the squadron strength, number of planes fit for combat, the amount of gasoline and ammunition on hand, and other information of primary importance.

At all hours of the day and night messages, often pages long, came pouring in from headquarters. One such dispatch, covering nearly half a typewritten page, when decoded, read: "ALERT ALL PURSUITS."

It was the notification for which we had been waiting. In five minutes, we had fourteen planes fully armed, manned with props spinning and on the line with noses pointing into the wind. The pilots, checking last minute instrument adjustments, were tense. When their radio headphones gave the order, they took to the air in rapid-fire succession.

The mission was intercepting Japanese bombers over Clark Field, a distance of ten air miles from our base. A range of mountains interfered with our view of the aerial activity and all we could do was to await the return of the fighters.

After fifteen minutes a sputtering drone announced the return of the first homecoming ship. The P-40 is normally flown onto its runway at a landing speed of one hundred and ten miles per hour, but this wounded bird, minus the use of three cylinders, limped in at about eighty miles per hour.

The uninjured pilot had just begun to relate the details of the fight when another ship came into land. The second plane had been riddled through the fuselage with fifty-caliber machine gun fire, but was still intact.

The pilot had come back for ammunition and another set of headphones; the ones he wore had been pierced through the right earpiece by a machine-gun bullet! For the following hour the planes arrived and departed. When the last pilot returned, he described the fate of the three missing ships.

One had crashed head-on into a Jap bomber, and the other two had been shot down in flames after having accounted for a number of enemy planes. That evening at dusk, we held a simple memorial service for the heroes who had died that day. Just a few words from the C.O., a moment of silence, and that was all; yet, of the men present that evening, the handful still living will never forget it. I know that I shall not.

The following morning two of our pilots flew on a reconnaissance mission to the northern tip of Luzon. One returned and told of his partner's plane having been shot down over wild mountainous terrain by Jap Zero-fighters. The unfortunate pilot was known to the men as "Red" because he had dyed his hair a crimson hue after losing a bet on a West Coast football game shortly before our departure from the States.

The fellow pilot on the mission-related having seen "Red" bail out of his ship, but the mountainous country was known to be inhabited by headhunters, and his chances of survival were slim.

Five days later, a strange looking individual rode onto the airstrip on the back of a water buffalo. The black whiskers were alien to us, but the flaming red hair could be none other than "Red's!" He told an exciting story of landing in the treetops near a village of savages.

The Philippine Constabulary[7] had warned these primitive natives to be on the alert for descending Japanese airmen, and they approached the falling parachutist with upraised spears. Fortunately, he thought of his red hair and, tearing off his helmet, pointed to the rufous locks and shouted, "Americano!"

---

[7] The Philippine Constabulary was the chief US law enforcement organization in the Philippines established after the islands were ceded to America following the Spanish-American War of 1898.

After spending the night with the savages, he hired a guide with a water buffalo which cost him his watch, class ring, and automatic pistol but proved to be a good investment as the day following his return to the base he was flying again.

All night, the ground crews worked preparing our remaining ships for combat flight. At 1 A.M. radio orders arrived and directed a strafing and personnel bombing mission at Lingayen Gulf where eighty Japanese troop transports were scheduled to land at dawn that morning.

Just as the first ray of dawn appeared over the mountain range, our remaining eleven planes took off on their deadly mission. Two hours later, when the air was split by a roar announcing their return, we looked skyward, observing the formation perfect except for one position: the lead plane was not in the flight. Even before the pilots had the opportunity to explain how it had happened, we knew that the Squadron Commander was missing.

The returning ten pilots described how they had strafed and bombed practically all of the eighty ships in the bay, causing tremendous havoc, and how the C.O. had dived his plane to within a few feet of a ship carrying ammunition on her foredeck. The bullets from his aerial machine guns had set off the munition dump and had torn the wings from his plane.

There could be no question about his death, as time did not permit his bailing out of the ship, and the tremendous rate of speed at which it plunged into the China Sea caused it to sink immediately. One of the greatest pilots and finest men I have ever met became an unsung hero in a watery grave.

By December 15, 1941, we wondered why our field had not been attacked by Japanese aircraft. Surely the enemy was aware of its existence as they had a well-founded espionage system informing their authorities of major positions and movements of American troops.

We learned from our military intelligence that all enemy planes were now based on Formosa. Although landings had been affected at several points on Luzon, air bases as yet had not been established on the island. We had been accurately informed that enemy pilots were poor night fighters, and, in conducting a mission in the Philippines, left their Formosan bases each morning, arriving at their targets not before 10 A.M.

Even when carrying reserve fuel in belly tanks, they were forced to depart for their fields before 2 P.M. to assure their arrival by nightfall.

Thus, from 2 o'clock in the afternoon until 10 o'clock the following morning, we felt comparatively safe from aerial attacks.

Several units of tank and infantry organizations had established a line to the north retarding the advance of enemy ground operations. Promptly at 10 o'clock one morning a roar filled the air. Our planes were all in revetments or hidden in a nearby patch of sugar cane, and we knew instantly that it was an attack.

Fortunately, most of the men were near the edge of the field and sought the protection of tropical trees. On either side of the main runway we had machine gun emplacements which were manned night and day. All of these gun positions opened fire in unison; their bursts, mingling with the roar of the strafing planes, made a tremendous noise.

For fifteen minutes they made run after run, their bullets setting several trucks and gasoline trailers afire; but their major objective appeared to be personnel, as they combed the brush on either side of the field repeatedly.

I, attempting to crawl under my steel helmet, was lying face down beside a friend. Suddenly, a bullet was deflected from my headgear with a resounding "ping."

I must have whimpered or made some sort of sound as the fellow next to me was certain that I had been hit. It took a full minute for him to muster up enough courage to shake me gently and to ask, "Reynolds, did they get you?" It was not my day, but for the duration of the campaign I wore that neatly creased helmet.

All but three of our fighter planes were damaged beyond repair in that raid. The senior flying officer, who had assumed command of the squadron after the death of the C.O., ordered all of the men, with the exception of a skeleton ground and communication crew, to evacuate the field for the nearby village of Del Carmen.

Twenty of us were left on the field, and the rest of the men moved into the luxurious cottages of the Spreckle Sugar Central in the village. There was little work for the squadron now. Men in the village guarded entrances to the town, and at the field we manned our communications dugout, manned anti-aircraft machine guns and kept a ground crew alerted to service any planes that might land.

Our disabled ships were placed on a make-believe takeoff line and from the air looked serviceable. Often Jap bombers en route to Manila with a lethal cargo of destruction dropped bombs on our decoys.

The tank cars used to transport molasses from the sugar refinery to the airstrip were on tracks alongside the field and were mistaken by Jap fighters for fuel cars. No doubt they wondered why their tracer bullets failed to set them ablaze. Our attempts to draw quantities of enemy fire' and bombs were more than successful.

I have mentioned the enemy's well-founded system of espionage. We were aware of its existence and trusted no Filipino. One afternoon in the communication dugout, I was talking on the field telephone with the first sergeant, who was in the village. During the conversation we both detected sounds of the wires being tapped and knew that somewhere along the line someone was listening in.

Of course, neither of us said anything over the wire regarding the eavesdropper, but in closing I mentioned something about making a trip into the village and in reply he stated that perhaps he would come out to the field. With tacit understanding I followed the telephone line from the field toward town, and he immediately checked the line from the town to the field.

Being a younger man and having less dense undergrowth to contend with, I made better time than the first sergeant. At a point a little further than half-way to the village, the line ran through a tall patch of sugar cane. Upon entering the patch, I heard someone thrashing his way through the head-high stalks. With automatic pistol in hand, I proceeded stealthily along the wire until I found a section that had unquestionably been scraped of insulation. A crude jackknife lay beside the bared strands.

Since effective pursuit through the cane was impossible, I proceeded along the wire, pretending not to have noticed the tampering. About fifty feet from the tapping I stopped, crawling cautiously back on my hands and knees, expecting the possible saboteur to return. I was lying in wait when the first sergeant arrived along the wire. He will never know how close he came to being shot that day!

On Christmas Day, 1941, USAFFE ordered the squadron to take up operations in a village called Orani on the northern tip of Bataan. Daytime road convoys were hazardous, to say the least, so we postponed the trip until evening. Perhaps another reason for our willingness to wait was the Spreckle Sugar Central's invitation to the squadron to eat dinner in their luxurious dining hall.

There in the wilds of Pampanga[8] the men of the organization enjoyed their last real meal together. Nothing was lacking as the traditional Christmas menu included imported foods, beer and liquors. At midnight, when we departed for Bataan,[9] the true spirit of Christmas reigned, and that bond, that intangible something that only fighting men know, made us feel more like brothers than fellow soldiers.

Prior to our evacuation of Del Carmen, in compliance with USAFFE instructions, we abandoned all of our personal equipment, as well as such luxuries as folding cots and mattresses.

Before relinquishing my trunk, which contained nearly all of my worldly treasures, I indulged in a gratifying last look at the pictures of my parents and loved ones, fully realizing that I would never see the pictures again, and also wondering if I would ever see the people portrayed.

---

[8] In central Luzon.
[9] In the southwest region of Pampanga.

3 - The Battle of Bataan

Orani, as we discovered the following morning, proved to be a typical Filipino fishing village located on Manila Bay. It had a grass-shack population of about fifteen hundred people, a few stores on the highway, and the customary marketplace. Near the center of the town was a public school, guarded by the traditional statue of José Rizal, the liberator of the Philippines,[10] and a beautiful fifteenth-century Spanish Catholic church.

Men of the squadron moved into the school and set up flight operations on the edge of town. This was indeed the most unusual landing field I have ever seen as it appeared to be nothing more than acres of old rice paddies, partitioned off in fifty-foot patches by earthen walls two feet high.

From the air it resembled a checker-board and just another rice field, but it had been so converted that the walls could be moved in a minimum of time, allowing planes to take off and land on a three-hundred-yard runway. As soon as our ships took to the air, the dirt walls were replaced until they returned. Little wonder that the Japs never did find our base, although they were certain that we were operating from somewhere near the village.

When the ships were on the ground, they were rolled under the protective foliage of a group of huge mango trees. Our precious remaining ships were being used for occasional interception and reconnaissance missions. For the following two weeks, we were visited daily by enemy aircraft. Observation planes took detailed pictures of the area, and dive-bombers combed the vicinity for signs of military activity.

By now the Japs had occupied Manila and had established air bases in and around the city. All of the American forces had evacuated to Bataan.

---

10 José Protasio Rizal Mercado y Realonda, 1861-1896; executed by Spanish authorities for inciting rebellion.

The Japs, in anguish over their failure to locate our position of operation, pattern-bombed the village, practically demolishing it.

Hundreds of natives were killed in their homes and bamboo air raid shelters. As soon as the bombers departed, the entire squadron searched the ruins for the injured, then returned to remove the dead.

It was a heartbreaking sight: fathers holding the mutilated bodies of babies in their arms, unable to comprehend that they were dead, little children with limbs torn off, and weeping families searching for loved ones. We cleaned up the gruesome mess as best we could, dressed the wounds of the injured, attempted to identify and bury the dead, and then advised the remaining villagers to evacuate the settlement for the protection of the neighboring mountains and forests.

When it seemed that the last family had left the village, someone discovered, crawling through the debris, a silly little puppy with sharply-pointed ears.

We fed him until it appeared he would burst, then began to think of a suitable name for him. When someone suggested "P-40" and the dog responded, he was so christened then and there.[11] In spite of his appearance, P-40 proved to be a smart pup. When planes approached, the dog made a mad dash for the nearest foxhole, and sweated out the raid with the men. Later when food became scarce, P-40 lived on frogs and wildflowers.

When toward the end of the campaign P-40 disappeared, an investigation revealed that he had been lured to the bivouac of a Filipino unit and barbecued.

On the same afternoon that P-40 was found in the wreckage, I was searching for bodies in the ruined buildings and while so doing found a case of American beer under a tremendous pile of debris. When I returned to our quarters with the case of beer under one arm and the body of a dead Filipino child under the other, the first sergeant inquired if I was

---

[11] After the Curtiss P-40 Warhawk attack plane.

acquainted with army regulations regarding looting during time of war.

I replied that I was, but that I considered this a lucky find; not looting.

"And besides," he said, "how are we going to chill it?" (Note that "we.")

That night at dusk, when our gory work was finished and the blood was washed from our hands and clothing, I made another trip into what was left of the village in search of a cake of ice.

In a former fish warehouse, I found a fifty-pound chunk and was returning when I met two Filipinos. They were carrying a pole between them on their shoulders, suspended from which were a few pots and pans and a huge pig, tied belly-up by its hocks. I asked where they were going, and in reply was told, "We are going to the mountains, sir. Thees place ees unsafe!"

There was nothing left of the village but ashes and splinters, and these men had finally decided that it was unsafe!

After I had chipped the ice and covered a washtub full of beer bottles with it and a couple pounds of salt, the first sergeant apologized for having accused me of looting, and readily accepted my invitation to help drink it. All was peaceful that night. The beautiful tropical moon shone through the banana trees and starlight filtered through the palms.

I tuned a portable radio to the now Japanese-controlled radio station in Manila broadcasting to the Americans on Bataan and dedicating such songs to us as "I'm Waiting for Ships That Never Come In," and "I'll Be Glad When You're Dead, You Rascal, You." Japan's 1941 version of Tokyo Rose[12] ended the program by saying softly, "Boys, are you sleeping with someone you love tonight? ... I am!"

The next day, between bombing and strafing attacks, we gathered up our equipment and, as per radio instructions

---

[12] The notorious female Japanese radio persona spouting discouraging lies to any Allied serviceman in the Pacific who happened to be listening; a media propaganda tactic borrowed from the British who employed broadcaster William Joyce to taunt Germans over the airwaves as 'Lord Haw-Haw.'

from USAFFE, now located on Corregidor, prepared to retreat further down the Bataan peninsula.

We were forced to wait until nightfall before making any road movements and by the time we left we could hear the machine gun and artillery fire of the advancing ground troops of the enemy.

Most of that night we drove over treacherous roads with the headlights of our cars and trucks blacked out. Our destination was Agaloma Point, on the extreme southern tip of the peninsula, where we were to assume duty as beach defense.

Our remaining three P-40s were flown to their last secret airstrip: Bataan Field. By the aid of crude maps and compass directions, we finally discovered the site of our ordered position. By the time we had set up our scant mess equipment and each man had cleared a place to sleep on the jungle floor, it was daylight.

After two hours of rest, we examined the beach to ascertain what installations would be required to fortify it against invasion.

We discovered a sheltered bay with a white sand shoreline and a point of land jutting out into the China Sea on either side. It was a heavenly place, resembling scenes in travelogues. Resolved to explore the south point, three friends and I cut our way through the jungle for two hours before reaching its terminus; a precipice seventy-five feet from the water's edge.

Looking down to the beach, we were amazed to see a huge rock about the size of a living room in an average American home. There was nothing unusual in that, but the rock was snow white in color! Closer examination revealed that our suspicions were correct; the rock had been painted, and a brush still lay alongside. There was no doubt in our minds that the Japanese had selected this point as a beach-head position for a landing attack. By the end of the day, we had the rock painted a dull green and had made splendid progress in the installation of machine-gun positions on both points and on the beach.

For the following two days we worked like mad, stringing barbed wire and installing heavier gun emplacements. From the Navy department at Mariveles we "borrowed" a three-inch all-purpose rifle for use on the south point. To make the installation we first had to clear a road through three miles of jungle to facilitate a caterpillar's towing it into position, but in a week, all was in readiness.

Not only was it a beautiful piece but a deadly one, having a range of several miles and a tremendous supply of ammunition. In the following weeks this weapon accounted for thousands of enemy lives.

By now our food supply was practically exhausted and we were solely dependent on the Quartermaster Corps to supply us with such luxuries as bread and canned vegetables. Each day, a pickup truck was sent to the QM dump, and our two meals per day were becoming scant. As our guns and defense equipment had all been installed, we arranged an eight-hour shift over a twenty-four-hour clock to man gun positions and lookout posts constantly.

On the night of January 15, 1942, the squadron was sleeping peacefully, with the exception of thirty men on watch at the beach, when things began to happen. The air was filled with machine-gun fire and rifle shots, which awakened us from sound slumber. Everyone, grabbing his weapons and helmet, made a mad dash for the beach, for we instantly knew what had happened. The Japs were making a landing!

While we were making our way to the beach, tripping over vines and windfalls, an alien sound reached our ears; something dull and hollow resembling mortar fire. Yes, it was; and we had no mortars! We quickly learned upon arrival at the beach that the landing had been affected on the north point. The night being dark and the restless ocean surf noisy, a comparatively easy task for the sneak invaders was possible.

Before being discovered and repulsed by our beach installations, at least twelve barge-loads of the enemy's men and equipment had successfully landed and made short work of our three men posted on the end of the point.

We quickly formed a line to hold the Japs on the peninsula and then began to advance to the point of contact. Rifle combat work was new to every man in the squadron. Most of the men knew nothing of the use or care of their newly-acquired equipment, but they learned quickly: the hard way.

For the following three weeks, we fought day and night in an attempt to regain possession of the point. With the aid of aerial support our task would have been much easier, but enemy planes were king of the air, and bombed and strafed advantageously. Two days following the night landing party, three enemy dive-bombers circled over the Jap ground troops for ten minutes, obviously in radio communication with them. At the conclusion of this spot flying, they dropped supplies in parachutes, which landed temptingly close to our line.

We vowed that the next time such provisions were dropped they would fall behind our lines. That night we made a costly advance, gaining about seventy-five yards. The following morning the Jap planes again appeared on their now daily mission, dropping six parachutes which we promptly recovered. Each chute was loaded with emergency rations: Hershey chocolate bars, Lucky Strike cigarettes, prayer books, and small caliber ammunition. The ammunition and prayer books we sent to the rear echelon for military intelligence to study. The rations, chocolate bars, and cigarettes we kept for our own analysis, for by this time we were truly hungry; thus, we learned that by advancing each night we were almost certain of "Bundles from Japan" the following morning.

Early one evening, a seven-man reconnaissance squad advanced on the left flank in an attempt to ascertain the source of the enemy's water supply. Deep in enemy territory, they discovered a group of Japs drinking and washing at a small spring emerging from the side of a cliff. They exchanged shots with these would-be washers, then retreated to their own lines.

That night we pushed our position to the left and gained possession of their only source of drinking water. The remaining Japs fought for the next seventeen days without water. Six days following the enemy's landing operation, we contacted an artillery unit which transported mobilized 155-mm. pieces to within three miles of the point and dropped unrelenting barrages of fire on the enemy day and night.

With the aid of this artillery, advance for the squadron was made much less perilous, as the enemy was forced to seek the protection of foxholes to evade the cutting shrapnel. During our now steady advance, we were surprised at not finding a single Japanese corpse. We later learned that all bodies were burned nightly on huge pyres. A Jap soldier would risk his life to recover the body of a comrade who was unmistakably dead.

At the time when we thought we might regain full possession of the point, we were visited by another enemy landing party. They came in on a dark, moonless night in alarming numbers; their method of invasion being the towing of barges of men and equipment by tugs to within fifty yards of the beach, then cutting them loose to drift in to shore.

Not a man was asleep that night, however, and we heard the approaching tugs with their sinister cargo in tow. The moment the tugs set free their burdens and returned to the awaiting troop transports out at sea, we cut loose on the drifting barges with every weapon we had.

Tracer bullets from thirty and fifty-caliber machine-guns lit the scene with a spectral red glow. When one of our tracers detonated a barge of ammunition, the entire beach flamed with white-hot light. In less than ten minutes, we killed at least fifteen hundred Japs. Those few who left their barges for the protection of the water were quickly accounted for by the sharks that infested these waters.

When dawn came, partially dismembered bodies gently surged on the beach in the changing tide. Overturned and still smoldering barges drifted like apparitions a few yards from shore, and the water was a pinkish hue with an occasional shark's fin seen slicing through it.

Sons of Nippon had gone to their reward. Although this remark may appear cynical, "reward" is the proper word for their end.

While living with the Japanese army in following months, I learned a war creed, memorized and recited by the Emperor's soldiers prior to their departure to a battle area. Translated, the canticle expresses, "This day I have been called by my

Emperor, through the grace of God, to fight for the land of my ancestors. If I go by sea, let my corpse be water-soaked. If I go by land, let my corpse be grass-grown. I will die for the Sovereign State; I will never turn back."

Toward the end of the Agaloma campaign, many Japs, faced with defeat, chose the "water-soaked" dividend by stripping down to nothing but a G-string and swimming straight out into the China Sea with the receding tide.

The first few we shot at like bottles on a mill pond, but later merely kept an eye on them through a telescope until a shark or exhaustion claimed them. Incidentally, when we shot at them, the suicide-bent Japs made no attempt to avoid our fire by zig-zagging their course or diving.

In pressing our advance against the remaining Japs on the point, we captured two of their number. As none of us spoke their language, we gained no information from them; but even if we had been able to talk with them, it would have been of little benefit as their mouths and tongues were swelled pitifully from lack of water.

We escorted the prisoners to the rear and gave them fresh water in minute quantities to prevent them from foundering themselves. After an hour, when their maddening thirst had subsided, we offered them cigarettes, which they shyly accepted. One had a nasty wound in his right shoulder, obviously many days old from the appearance of the bloody rag covering it. One of our medical men cut away the bandage to inspect the wound, and we were horrified to find it swarming with maggots. When the squadron doctor arrived on the scene, he seemed quite calm while observing our nauseating discovery. He proceeded to remove the larvae, cleanse the wound and dress it with sulfa powder and fresh gauze.

He informed us that in the absence of disinfecting agents, the presence of this carnivorous larvae is a splendid precaution against gangrene and similar infections, as they consume the rotting flesh but do not eat the living tissue. In the months to come we found his theory correct when we too were confronted with infectious wounds. We sent the prisoners to the rear, where a prisoner-of-war stockade had been established. There they were interrogated at length, then confined.

Our fighting had now become almost routine as the enemy was weakening, and we suffered few casualties. After an eight-hour shift on the line, we were relieved by fresh men and had the next twelve hours off. However, most of these hours were spent in the hunting and cooking of food. I'm afraid we weren't very good sportsmen, hunting wild boar with automatic weapons; but when the gnawing pains of hunger urge one in the pursuit of game, the sportsman's code of ethics is easily forgotten.

One day my buddies and I slept before our hunting expedition and about two hours before time to return to the line, I awakened. Because the other fellows were sleeping soundly for the first time in weeks, I hated to disturb them. Slipping back into the jungle, I returned in less than an hour with a luscious young boar, riddled in nine places with automatic-rifle fire.

After we had dressed the animal, it was time to return to our position on the front again, but that would mean not eating the boar, for in the tropics meat begins to decay as soon as it is killed.

We took the dressed carcass to the line with us that evening, built a fire and slowly turned it on a spit. It was a very reckless thing to do, since many Japs undoubtedly saw the flame. Maybe they thought it was a trick to draw their fire because they did not attempt to ascertain its reason for being.

At any rate, we cooked the animal to perfection and thoroughly enjoyed the meal. I have often looked back on that night, realizing how reckless we had been, making silhouettes of ourselves before an open fire, but hungry men are willing to risk untold dangers to appease their appetites.

Often, when wild boar were difficult to find, we ate monkeys. Although the meat of the monkey is sweet and tender, I dreaded seeing one of the harmless creatures dressed; they so resembled a human baby that it made me sick. Often while I was on a hunting expedition, the other fellows prepared a meal of monkey meat. Having missed the unappetizing sight of dressing the monkey, I thought an arm or leg of the little animal tasted pretty good. Boa constrictor and python were very elusive prey, but the few we managed to kill provided excellent meat.

Our chief standby for off-duty meals was fish. Having no fishing tackle, we used dynamite with wonderful results. One stick of the explosive, detonated in the right spot, accounted for about a dozen fish. This system worked splendidly until we exhausted our supply of dynamite. We experimented with hand grenades but found with their fifteen-second fuses they produced poor results.

To one not familiar with the mechanics of grenades, here is an explanation of their workings. When using a grenade, one pulls the pin from the handle, then throws it. Fifteen seconds after the pin has been removed, the grenade explodes with tremendous force, throwing shrapnel in all directions. When used for blasting fish, the grenade reached the ocean bottom before the fifteen-second exploding time had expired. As the force of the blast goes down in water, the results were poor.

We reasoned that, if one held the grenade in his hand for eight or ten seconds before throwing it into the water, it would detonate a few feet below the surface, thus stunning all the fish under it. In theory this idea was correct, but in practice we found a spitting grenade a difficult object to hold in our hands, trying to guess at what moment it would explode.

Necessity being the mother of invention, however, we soon contrived a device consisting of a block of wood with three feet of string attached. To the end of the string we tied the live grenade, throwing the entire apparatus into the water. The block prevented the missile from sinking too deeply before it exploded. Our fishing worries were over; that is, until we ran out of hand grenades.

Although we now had the fighting situation under control, the morale of the entire squadron was dangerously low. We had lost a number of men, there was a critical shortage of food, and many of the men continually scanned the horizon, vainly watching for the help which was never to arrive from the States.

Our daily ration allowance from the Quartermaster Corps ran something like this: one-third of a sack of rice, four cans of sardines, three cans of evaporated milk, two pounds of sugar, and a pound of coffee; this was to suffice the needs of the entire squadron of one hundred and eighty men. Through great effort, our mess sergeant managed to serve one meal per day, consisting of nothing but a cup of slum, made of rice, a little fish, less sugar, and a few wild greens picked in the jungle. Our scant cavalry had long since been eaten, giving each organization on Bataan a quarter cut of meat. My squadron drew the front quarter of a pack mule, made up largely of bone and hide.

Three o'clock each afternoon was our dinner hour. At that time gun positions were manned by skeleton crews, and most of the organization was together. On one such afternoon, as we were feasting, three of our pilots were called from the area by a motorcycle messenger. They returned in a few minutes with a sealed envelope, exchanged happy looks among themselves, then looked at us with the expression of the family cat after having eaten the goldfish.

Upon completion of their meal, they departed in an old convertible Buick sedan that someone had picked up on our evacuation of the sugar central. No one knew what their orders were, but we did know that USAFFE had three pursuit planes at the secret Bataan airstrip. We were certain they had been ordered on some sort of mission and discovered the nature of it the following day. The next morning when the three Japanese dive-bombers circled overhead, as usual, above their trapped ground troops, we detected a high-pitched drone above the purr of the Jap ships.

Looking high in the sky, we saw three dots about three thousand feet above the enemy planes. After each pilot picked his target, the P-40s rocketed in 9-G dives toward the bombers. We watched the maneuver breathlessly, not daring to whisper in fear of the Jap pilots hearing us, which was, of course, ridiculous, when three sets of aerial machine-guns spat simultaneously, and the three Jap planes were hit. One crashed in flames, another glided dead-stick into the China Sea, and the third crashed into the side of a mountain two miles away. The P-40's buzzed our group, dipping their wings, and then they were returned to the airstrip. Those three aerial victories had raised our morale three hundred percent!

The Japanese ships' failure to return to their base must have caused untold consternation as we were reported to have had no airplanes left on Bataan. Later that day, three more Jap bombers arrived on the scene at the same altitude as their predecessors, obviously awaiting a similar attack, and high above them were a dozen Zero fighters, partially concealed by the clouds.

No attack came, however, as our planes were safely hidden away in the jungle and our pilots were back with us, looking up through the foliage and laughing. We estimated that there were about two hundred weakened enemy troops left on the point, and that the time was ripe for the final mop-up operation. We advanced our line as far forward as possible, dug new trenches and foxholes, installed machine-gun emplacements and then sent a platoon of men around on the right flank to drive the Japs toward us. Everything worked as had been planned, the enemy being driven into our fire like deer driven from a swamp toward posted riflemen.

If enemy aircraft had not appeared on the scene, we would have suffered practically no casualties. Most of our men had the advantageous protection of the jungle and could keep up a steady volley of fire without being seen from the air, but a buddy and I had the misfortune of being located on a high point of sandy soil without a tree or bush within fifty feet.

As the Japs came rushing toward us, we maintained a steady rain of fire on them, dropping them in their tracks. When the enemy planes spotted our position, we could not cease fire because their advancing troops would be upon us in seconds; nor could we raise our machine-gun even momentarily. The Zeros made four runs, strafing our emplacement. On their last run my comrade and I, lying flat on our bellies, kept our fire dead-ahead. Little splashes of sand appeared around and between us where the planes' bullets hit.

Until now not a word had been spoken between us as we grimly grasped our weapon in a determined effort to kill as many Japs as possible before we were killed. Suddenly my partner broke the spell by saying, "Golly, Reynolds, I believe those guys are trying to kill us!"

It was not our day to die. The final operation was gory but fast. We proceeded to burn the bodies of the dead Japs and to salvage as much of their combat equipment as possible.

When the first bodies on the pyre began to burn and explosions occurred, we realized that most of the Japs carried hand grenades in their pockets; consequently, we were forced to search each body prior to its cremation. In so doing we found many odd trinkets, including watches and rings bearing English inscriptions, obviously taken from British soldiers killed or captured at Singapore.

The malodorous stench of burning flesh leaves an indelible impression on one's mind not quickly forgotten. The Japanese attempted one more landing at Agaloma Beach.

Just as the sun was dropping into the China Sea one evening, an observer on a BC-scope discovered an enemy cruiser and a troop transport lying about twenty-five thousand yards out in the sea. A full view of the vessels was obstructed by the earth's curvature. We noted their inactivity, and were certain of their plans. After nightfall, they would slip closer in toward shore, where the cruiser would shell our beach installations.

Under the protective fire of the cruiser, the troop transport would dispatch men in barges to affect a beachhead. We notified the airstrip of our discovery and suggested that three of our pilots be sent to the field so they would be ready in the event that we needed aerial support in resisting the invaders. As the pilots left, they called, "We'll see you about midnight."

We did. At 11 P.M., the first round of shellfire resounded from the cruiser, now about five thousand yards out to sea. In the following hour and a half, about a hundred rounds were fired from the man-of-war.

Their fire was inaccurate, thus ineffective. It succeeded in keeping us near the protection of foxholes most of the time; but when the sound of tugs announced the arrival of troop-carrying barges, gaining access to the beach, every weapon on our points cut loose. When the landing operation began, a radio operator contacted the airstrip where our three planes with props turning were waiting on the runway. In less than five minutes we ceased our ground fire and watched the deadly work of the planes diving on the now-flaming barges.

The pilots took turns in making runs; each run consisted of a thousand-foot seventy-degree angle dive, all guns blazing. As every fourth round of ammunition in their aerial machine-gun belts was a tracer, the scene was clearly lit.

Not a Jap set foot on shore that night, and the sharks had another good meal, for the barges that drifted into the shore were all empty.

Three days following the last attempted landing, the commanding officer sent a messenger to our gun position to summon me. I couldn't imagine what I had done.

A couple of weeks previously, three other fellows and I had participated in an unauthorized Jap sniper hunt, using twelve-gauge shotguns (contrary to rules of warfare according to International Law). Incidentally, we got the sniper, too. I didn't think that the "old man" had gotten wind of that escapade, however. I felt relieved when he explained the purpose of his consultation.

Our squadron sergeant-major at Group Headquarters on the foot of Mariveles Mountain had been sent to the field hospital, and I was to take over his job. That afternoon I said "Goodbye" to the boys, mounted a motorcycle, and proceeded to my new station. I hated to leave the old gang but found my new work much less nerve-wracking.

My duties were simple, consisting of squadron reports to USAFFE Headquarters, keeping in touch with the squadron by walky-talky, and tending to its administration and status needs. An occasional flight of enemy planes dropped its cargo near our area in attempting to demolish a navy pier nearby, but other than that things were pretty quiet.

On the first day at my new station I was working in front of a typewriter while wearing headphones. Suddenly everyone in the tent dropped his work and fell face-down on the ground. Naturally, I removed my headphones and asked what was wrong.

"Enemy planes overhead!" they shouted. "Get down on the floor, you fool!"

I complied with their bidding. The poor fellows were shaking with fear, expecting to be bombed out of existence at any moment. Then I understood their logic. They had never seen any action but had been dodging bombing raids for months. Naturally, their nerves were on edge. At Agaloma that sort of thing occurred constantly, and we had even become accustomed to being shot at without suffering any undue alarm.

I must have been considered a cold-blooded individual; but nevertheless, after having been through what I had, and while thinking of the boys in the squadron down at the beach, I just couldn't find myself becoming excited when a flight of Jap ships happened to pass overhead.

I spent much of my off-duty time in the surrounding jungle hunting for iguana. Meat from the tail of the iguana proved to be tastier roast chicken than any wild boar or python I had eaten; still I couldn't help but recall having seen them feasting on the bloated bodies of dead Japs on the beach at Agaloma.

In the area surrounding our bivouac were trees bearing fruit identical to the bell pepper, but bright yellow in color, and from the bottom hung a half-moon-shaped shell. Further investigation revealed them to be cashew nuts. The delicious fruit contained sweet juice, resembling nothing I had ever tasted. The nuts embodied an acid which burned one's flesh if not cooked before eating. We contrived a method of roasting the nuts by placing them, shell and all, into a mess kit held above a fire. When heated, they exuded a light oil to which we in turn set fire.

Soon the entire contents of the pan were flaming; but when the flames died out, the nuts were perfectly roasted and made a tasty morsel. Salt was a rare delicacy and the little we had was procured from boiled-down seawater. The finished product was a wet, brown mass, looking like anything but salt and having a mineral taste. Nevertheless, it was sodium chloride and made our meager rations more palatable.

A former Manila merchant, a Chinese jokingly called "Tin Pan Sam" by the men, had taken refuge with his family in a shack on the Mariveles River. Sam made weekly trips to Manila in a dugout to purchase black market articles which he in turn sold for exorbitant prices to the men on Bataan. However, his high price was probably justified because he not only had to paddle his frail craft over forty miles of Manila Bay but would have lost his head had he been apprehended in Jap-occupied Manila.

One afternoon as an accommodation, Sam sold two other fellows and me a gallon of pancake batter for two hundred dollars.

We had our mouths set for a batch of golden-brown hotcakes, but had forgotten the necessity of grease in which to fry them. We tried motor oil on the griddle but got poor results. Someone produced a jar of Vaseline, but that didn't taste good either.

Finally, a medical man gave us a small bottle of mineral oil which fried the cakes beautifully with no obnoxious taste. However, to our regret we learned that mineral oil performs its basic function whether taken by the spoonful or camouflaged in the form of hotcakes. We later learned to solve our grease-shortage problem by rendering oil from the fat found inside of iguanas and by storing it in tin cans for future use.

Late one afternoon, a radio message came from USAFFE which was in turn transmitted to my squadron at the beach. It contained orders for three of our pilots to report to the airstrip at dusk: Mission "Blackhawk."

After relaying the directive, I left an assistant in charge of my desk and checked the fuel supply on my motorcycle. It contained nearly a gallon of gas; and since the airstrip was only four kilometers away, I couldn't resist the impulse to see the ships off.

The pilots, looking like a group of college boys on the way to a football game rather than fighter pilots headed for a deadly mission, reached the field in their run-down Buick convertible almost as soon as I did on my vehicle.

Not until they were actually in the air did they open their sealed instructions for the raid. Those of us left on the field tried to play poker by candlelight for the next two hours while awaiting their return; but each time a mosquito buzzed, we dropped our cards, thinking it was the return of the flight.

Finally, the awaited roar came. Our hearing had become so keyed to the pitch of airplane motors that we could determine the number of ships in a flight. Yes, all three had returned! Ground crewmen flashed the field lights for an instant, guiding the planes in; and before the pilots could crawl from their cockpits, we had gathered around them for a report of the raid.

It was truly the most daring undertaking I had ever heard of. They had flown over Jap-occupied Manila to Nichols Field, which was, of course, blacked out. The lead pilot saw a tiny bead of light flicker down on the field, and not knowing just why, flashed his running lights for a bare second.

This was obviously the signal used by incoming Jap planes, as the entire field was immediately flooded with lights, giving our pilots an unobstructed view of a vast number of planes lined up on the runways. They made two fast runs, strafing and wing-bombing the entire field, before some Jap attendant had the presence of mind to extinguish the lights.

They returned with empty ammunition belts and bomb-racks without having been fired upon. No wonder we on Bataan were bombed for nine consecutive hours the following day!

During the lull of the following week, we were informed by the Jap-controlled radio station in Manila that General Masaharu Homma had ordered a half million of his troops to reinforce the Jap divisions now engaged in combat on Bataan and that all of the remaining American forces on the peninsula would be dead within ten days. They concluded their morale-breaking program with a recording of Chopin's "Funeral March."

There was little doubt in our minds but that they meant business. Two Japanese generals had already committed hari-kari over their failure to take Bataan, but it did not seem reasonable that the man who had directed attacks throughout the Southwest Pacific would lose face by failure to conquer a handful of Americans whose supplies and foodstuffs were practically nil. Two days after the major drive began, several men from the Thirty-first Infantry Division entered our area in their retreat from the front-line sector of Bataan, announcing that the line had been pierced by thousands of Japs.

Several hours later we were notified by USFIP,[13] having been changed from USAFFE after MacArthur's evacuation of the Philippines, to destroy all of our arms and ammunition in preparation for a mass surrender.

After we had demolished half of our equipment, the order was rescinded, yet we quietly continued to dump ammunition into the river and to spring rifle barrels out of line against tree trunks. Firing pins removed from sidearms rendered them useless.

For its combat work on Bataan, my squadron had been cited three times during three months by Presidential citation. We felt bitter about admitting defeat and were appalled by the thought of surrendering equipment to the Japs. Not a Jap soldier appeared on the scene that night.

We tried to sleep and yet couldn't help dreading the morning and what it might bring. About 2 A.M., I finally fell into an exhausted stupor, only to be rudely awakened to full consciousness shortly after by a tremendous thud. For the following three minutes the earth shook with violent convulsions, causing trees to sway and crack.

My first impression was that a gigantic ammunition dump must have been exploded, but the sound of an explosion was not to be heard. Thus, I experienced my first, but not last, earthquake. Even the elements seemed to be against us!

That morning we learned that our surrender had been unconditional in every respect. We were entirely at the mercy of our pagan foe. The first reconnaissance troops to enter our area were armed to the teeth. They asked for Camel cigarettes and cameras; all, of course, by gestures, such as pointing to a partially filled package of Camels and a cheap Jap camera. Needless to say, our meager supply of cigarettes had long since been smoked, and our cameras had been destroyed on

---

[13] United States Forces in the Philippines.

the previous night. Later that day, we were rounded up like a herd of cattle by a rough bunch of Jap soldiers with fixed bayonets and were driven into an old rice paddy four kilometers from Mariveles.

Just before leaving our former area, one of our officers produced a store of canned emergency rations which he had been saving for a rainy day. That the rainy day was at hand, we all agreed, and a count of the items revealed that we had just enough to give one can, large or small, regardless of what it might contain, to each man in the squadron.

Everyone agreed to accept whatever he drew, whether it be evaporated milk, corned beef, or what have you. Ten minutes later, I was fondling a can of Old Dutch Cleanser, wondering what to do with it and watching others puncturing cans and devouring their contents.

On our forced march to the rice paddies, where all of the American forces were being congregated, I witnessed the fate of the Japanese soldiers whom we had captured at Agaloma and those captured at other sectors.

The group of eleven was marched from the wire stockade to a clearing beside the road. There their hands were untied, each was given a cigarette, and then they were shot without further ceremony.

They weren't buried but were left in the field to rot in the tropical heat. Little wonder we were pessimistic about our future; it was evident that our captors had little respect for prisoners of war. The rice field on which we were assembled was about a mile square and had a stream running through the center of it.

When we arrived, the stream had been partitioned off as follows: the upper third had been roped off for the Japs' drinking water and bathing area; the center third was reserved for the Jap cavalry horses; the third portion was for the use of the American prisoners wishing to obtain drinking water and to bathe.

We stayed in this area for two days and on the evening of the second day, we were driven en masse onto the road once more and began the infamous Bataan Death March.

4 - The Death March

WE MARCHED THROUGHOUT THE NIGHT and all of the following day. Fortunately, most of us had filled our canteens prior to starting the march without realizing it would be our last drinking water for eight days. During the heat of the day many of the men, weakened from months of hunger and hardships, began to stagger and fall. Their fate was swift and merciless; they were merely escorted to the side of the road and were bayoneted through the back.

Many of the fellows attempted to help an unsteady comrade by placing an arm around him. As soon as such aid was discovered by the Japs, the weakened man was separated from his Samaritan and was administered the usual cold-steel treatment. We witnessed several instances where resistance was offered by the helping friend and both men were promptly killed. The psychological effect of knowing that a few faulty steps would result in instant death was maddening. On the entire march I heard but one shot fired, and that was in the case of a prisoner making a dash for the nearby jungle in an attempt to escape.

We would have marched all that next night had not a convoy of trucks carrying ammunition, men and mobilized artillery into Bataan for the assault on Corregidor demanded the entire road. Our procession was herded into a growing field of rice where stagnant, knee-deep water provided little refreshment because it had been fertilized by human excrement. Since this area had been planted with rice, it had served as a battlefield; consequently, the bloated bodies of men and animals lay partially submerged in the mire.

Upon entering the field, we were ordered into a column-of-four formation and remained standing in that position for the next nine hours. This was the way we "rested" during the night. At dawn the following morning, we were glad to continue our march to the north for we realized that, the sooner we ended this nightmarish ordeal, the better were our chances of survival.

As we passed through Filipino villages, artesian wells gushed cold water several feet into the air. At each well our guards paused momentarily, emptied their canteens into the dust of the road and refilled them with fresh water. They took delight in watching our thirst-craved expressions.

The sight of water being poured into the dirt was more than some of the men could stand and they, making a mad dash for the spot, were promptly bayonetted. Strangely enough, men bayonetted in this manner seldom emitted even a groan; only a gurgling sound as they dropped in their tracks, and a small trickle of blood could be seen oozing from their mouths. With the exception of an occasional roadside rest on our feet, we continued the march, day and night, for the following five days.

Naturally, no one could walk in the heat of the tropics for more than a day without water. Under the cover of darkness and the threat of death, we dipped our cups into the roadside ditches which were strewn with the decaying bodies of men and horses; occasionally we pressed our cups against one of these corpses.

Distasteful as this water was, it was still a liquid and without it we would all have died. Dysentery, diphtheria, cholera and typhoid contracted from the polluted water in many cases required weeks to manifest themselves and were a contributing factor in the thousands of deaths that occurred in prison camps following the Death March. When our procession approached a clearing called Cabcaben Field, we were packed into the area in a shoulder-to-shoulder sitting position. As soon as the entire field was filled with prisoners, a tremendous volley of artillery fire commenced directly behind us. We knew instantly what was taking place. The Japs had set up field pieces around us with which they would shell Corregidor, just a few miles out in Manila Bay.

They were confident that the Island Fortress would not return their fire and jeopardize the lives of thousands of American captives. After thirty minutes of the barrage, a single shot resounded from one of Corregidor's big guns, scoring a direct hit on one of the Jap gun emplacements. The shell landed inside the sandbag barricade set in a fifteen-foot diameter around the piece, blowing up gun, men and all.

Such marksmanship could not last, however, and the second round of fire from "The Rock" hit the edge of the clearing, spraying the vicinity with shrapnel.

About thirty men were killed or wounded by that one shell, and the remainder of us refused to sit and be killed without doing something about it. As we poured en masse onto the road, Corregidor continued its volley of shells.

Some of the men, including myself, began the march with light packs containing underclothing, a change of khakis, toilet articles, and a blanket; but as the march continued, we were stripped of all our possessions.

The Japanese had jungle-garrisons at ten-kilometer intervals along the road, and fresh sentries took charge of us at each encampment. As we passed each bivouac, hundreds of curious Japs would pour onto the road and search us for valuables. I had my wristwatch and my mother's graduation ring suspended from a cord around my neck, which escaped detection for four days, but finally a wary Jap discovered my hoard and, not being too cautious about the operation, slashed the cord with a saber.

On the sixth day of the march, we were too concerned about our lives to worry about being stripped of personal equipment. It was on that day that my final possession, the toothbrush that I carried in a pocket, was taken from me.

To many of the men, suicide seemed the only escape from this hideous ordeal of marching, especially in the cases of older fellows. Hardly a bridge was crossed from which someone did not dive headfirst onto the rocks far below as our lamentable procession continued its course northward.

Late in the afternoon of the seventh day, we were halted at a huge tin rice storehouse, where the men sought refuge in the empty building.

When the building was filled, the remainder of us made ourselves as comfortable as possible on the ground outside. It seemed apparent that we would spend the night here.

At the warehouse we learned that we had an interpreter in our midst; an American civilian who had been working with the army on Bataan, had spent seven years in Japan and spoke Japanese fluently. Through him we learned that the following day our march would end in a city called San Fernando, a distance of thirty-five kilometers.

That night, for the first time in days, we stretched out and tried to rest. I lapsed into a fitful slumber but was awakened by a shrill screaming in the middle of the night. By the light of a flaming torch, I saw four men bayoneted through the stomach, then dragged by the hair and thrown into a pit which thousands of men had used for a toilet.

Word quickly spread of what had happened. These men had swept up about a cupful of rice from the floor of the warehouse and had built a small fire under a shirt in an attempt to boil it in a canteen. A sentry had discovered the fire, stamped it out, and then "punished" the offenders. I wondered what the Japanese castigation would be for a second offense. No wonder our nerves were on edge; we never knew what minor infraction of rules might cause us to be the next killed.

The following morning, we set out on the last lap of the march and reached our destination late that afternoon. Nearly all of us were staggering from hunger and thirst by that time, and the Japs allowed us to assist one another for the first time.

Because our procession was about three miles long, only the first portion had been able to cross a narrow bridge before a convoy of trucks blocked the traffic for a half hour. When the convoy had passed, the remainder of the column was forced to run for the next hour in order to catch up with the forepart. While one was helping a sick friend, this double-timing was extremely difficult. Men who fell beside the road or lagged in the march were dealt with in the same swift, merciless manner as those at the beginning of the ordeal.

We must have been a ghastly-looking group of men to the Filipinos who lined the streets of San Fernando to see us. None of us had shaved or washed for a week, most of us were staggering, and many of the men mumbled incoherent phrases in their semi-delirium.

Here we were herded into the yard of the village school and were guarded by sentries, armed to the teeth, surrounding the enclosure. It was then that we assumed command of our own group and assembled into bodies of one hundred men.

A count at dusk revealed eighty such groups. Thirteen thousand Americans had started the Death March, and eight thousand had survived.

The prosecuting authorities in the trial of General Homma, charged with having ordered the Death March, produced evidence that seventeen thousand, two hundred American and Filipino captives lost their lives in this forced march that will live forever in infamy.

That night, for the first time since our capture, we were fed. Each man was given a cup of cooked rice and the same amount of water. I poured my water over the hot rice and then drank it. It was the most delicious soup I had ever tasted!

After the meal, I slept as I hadn't slept in weeks. With part of my morning ration of water, I wet a piece of shirt-tail and washed some of the grime from my face and hands. I felt much better after that and devoured my cup of rice with great relish.

At two o'clock that afternoon a Japanese officer entered the stockade, strode back and forth and looked over most of the group. He selected sixty men, who were placed under guard near the gate of the enclosure. I was one of those chosen, but for what purpose no one knew. It was obvious that we were going somewhere, so I called a quick "Goodbye" to the fellows remaining behind before climbing into one of the two awaiting trucks.

Standing beside each truck were three Jap guards who watched us mount and then handed up to us their rifles and bayonets while they climbed aboard.

The trucks left the curb and headed back toward Bataan.

5 – BACK TO BATAAN

FOR THREE HOURS WE RODE on the bouncing trucks in silence. The roadside was littered with the bodies of men, several of whom I recognized. A number of these corpses had not been dragged to the gutter and were being crushed by the wheels of our truck. But where could we be going, and for what purpose?

When the trucks halted in Balanga, Bataan, in front of two large native houses, we were ordered to dismount and to assemble in one of the front yards. A well-dressed Japanese officer appeared and looked us over from head to foot, counted us, then gave the guards a command in Japanese idiom which we did not understand. They snapped to attention, bowed, hissed their compliance, and motioned us into action. Our march lasted for ten minutes, ending on the banks of a shallow river, and, of course, we took over from there. There were gallons and gallons of fresh water for our dehydrated bodies to soak up.

We wallowed in the stream, drinking our fill and then washed our clothing. We would probably have stayed there for a week had not the guards ordered us out in an hour. All of us had shaggy beards, but our bodies were scrubbed clean with water and sand and our wet clothing hung from our arms.

When we returned, the officer again scrutinized us, looking much more pleased this time, and even managing to smile. We must have been a strange-looking lot! We were taken to our new quarters, two grass huts formerly occupied by Filipino villagers and now commandeered for our use.

After hanging our wet clothing from the rafters as best we could, we were summoned by a guard, who gestured that it was time to eat and wanted two men to go after the food.

The men returned with two buckets of rice and a dried fish per man. We thought we were being fed royally, and thoroughly enjoyed the meal. Night fell and while we were smoking the cigarettes the Japs had given us, a sentry assumed his post outside our flimsy quarters and announced in pantomime that it was time for us to sleep. We had no blankets, but most of our clothing was dry enough to wear during the night.

I awakened about midnight, found the room exceedingly stuffy, and took a chance on going outside for a breath of fresh air. It seemed that the sentries had changed since we retired because a strange young Jap was posted just outside our door.

As I left the shack, the guard, loosely carrying his rifle with fixed bayonet, approached me. About three feet away he stopped, looked me up and down and then stood by my side comparing our heights. After this he stepped back again, came smartly to attention by presenting arms and then proceeded to execute the Japanese version of the manual of arms.

When he finished, he slapped the rifle into my hands and gestured that I follow suit. Momentarily I was at a loss but quickly recalled some rifle training I had had at a military camp back in 1936 and did as good a job as I could for him. It must have met with his approval, for he grunted his satisfaction. I returned the rifle to him.

He back-stepped about eight feet, then lunged toward me with a bayonet thrust. I quickly stepped aside, not certain if he was still demonstrating the Jap method of rifle drill or had become blood-thirsty. When he again handed me his rifle to exhibit my version of bayonet routine, I showed him a trick I had learned on Bataan.

In executing this maneuver, one approaches his intended victim with bayonet extended; then at a crucial moment when the subject attempts to block the attack, he quickly swings the bayonet into the air, striking the butt of the rifle against his opponent's jaw. The Jap reacted perfectly to the trick, and I brought the rifle stalk to rest about an inch from his jaw. I could easily have knocked him out, had I wanted to. The Jap realized this and grinned at his own gullibility. For the next hour we sat outside of the shack and smoked his cigarettes. Regardless of the army of which one is a member, there is some sort of mutual veneration between one fighting man and another. Once having experienced actual combat, a soldier feels a respect for his enemy.

In the following years of prison life, when finding ourselves under the custody of new guards, we at once scanned their uniforms for campaign ribbons, knowing that our treatment would be more humane under battle-seasoned troops than in the hands of occupational forces who masqueraded under the laurels of combat soldiers.

The following morning, we heard for the first time, "Show, show," which in Jap army vernacular means time to get up. We washed at a nearby artesian well and then had breakfast, consisting once more of rice and dried fish. It seemed that the guards had already eaten because they loaded tools onto a truck while we were consuming our food.

That we were going to work was obvious, but, of course, we had no idea where. When we were ordered to board the trucks, we explained as best we could that four of our men were too sick to work; the Japs seemed to understand.

For two and a half hours, we rode south on the Bataan highway toward Mariveles. Judging from the constant flow of Japanese equipment into Bataan, we were certain that Correg-idor was still fighting.

As we rounded a curve in the road that gave us a clear view of the Island Fortress in Manila Bay, it was indeed a thrill to see Old Glory proudly flying from the center of the Fort. The Japs on the truck couldn't help but notice our delight at the sight, but made no comment. Near the city of Mariveles, a shell had torn up the road and halted traffic. With picks and shovels and crude litters, we filled in the cavity and proceeded down the road to where the approach of a bridge required the same repair.

At noon we were each given a cup of cold rice and a half can of sardines. It seemed wonderful to be eating regularly again! At the end of the day we returned to our quarters where we bathed again in the river, and after supper held a simple memorial service for the man who had died while we had been away working. The other three men who had remained in camp had washed the corpse and had attempted to dig a grave; but in so doing, one man collapsed from exhaustion. On our return they apologized for not having completed the dig-ging.

One fellow had just finished carving a neat cross for the man's grave. That was only the beginning of those evening ceremonies; for during the following month and a half, we lost twenty-one of our group of sixty men. The march from Bataan, together with hunger, malaria and dysentery, was too much for many of them to endure.

One morning after we had been in Balanga for five days, we prepared to go to work as usual but noticed little activity on the part of the Japs.

When told that this was a holiday and that there would be no work, we were pleased for our hands were badly blistered from working and we could use a day of rest nicely. Once more we bathed but did not feel thoroughly clean without shaving.

One of the Jap guards who lived a few shacks from our quarters had been quite friendly, and I wondered if he might not lend me a razor. I motioned to the sentry that I wanted to walk down the road a few yards, and, with a puzzled expression on his face, he followed me.

The soldier whom I had intended to ask for the loan of his razor was lying on a grass mat in the house, obviously sleeping, so I turned to leave. He shouted to me in Japanese and raised himself up on his elbow to inquire what I wanted.

He sounded quite gruff; but it was too late to turn back now, so I drew his attention to my beard and went through the motions of shaving. Without a word he arose, opened a bag, and produced a beautiful straight-edged razor, brush, soap and a leather strop.

When I returned to our area with the equipment, the fellows gasped. We all shaved that day and trimmed one another's necks. By noon we looked like a different group of men. From that time on, each day we had a holiday, I borrowed that same gear and we all enjoyed the luxury of a shave. However, as more and more of our number passed away, I found myself looking into that broken piece of mirror and saying to myself, "Well, Bob, another shave; wonder if this will be the last."

Each day on the ride to work we anxiously scanned Manila Bay for the sight of the American flag on Corregidor.

Unless help arrived soon, however, we knew that they couldn't hold out, as Japanese troops, mobilized artillery and landing equipment were thundering into Bataan day and night and "The Rock" was being shelled constantly by enemy gun emplacements, now advantageously located on Bataan.

As we repaired the damaged roads, shells from Corregidor screamed over us and at times landed so dangerously close that the Jap guards felt compelled to seek cover.

On May 7, 1942, we were greeted by the sight of the Japs' Rising Sun flying in the place of Old Glory on the fortress, and our last clinging hopes for freedom were shattered. Near the end of May, on one of our holidays, the Japs sent a truck to San Fernando and asked for four men to go along to load supplies. Three other fellows and I volunteered.

As we passed the tin rice warehouse, where we had spent our last night on the march from Bataan a familiar smell reached our nostrils; the pungent odor of decaying flesh. Later in the day, we learned from Filipinos in San Fernando that the men too sick to leave on the last lap of the march had been machine-gunned where they lay in the building.

After we had loaded the truck with dried fish and rice in the village, our driver headed for the public market place. There, the guards left the truck, instructing us not to dismount, and they entered one of the buildings.

The Filipinos, seeing us unguarded, tossed bananas, pineapples, cocoanuts, candy and cigarettes onto the truck. We tried to conceal our loot from the guards when they returned; but because we had a burlap sack full, it was rather difficult. They obviously didn't notice our precious bundle, that is, until we neared our quarters once more. When the truck stopped, they gestured for us to unload our stuff quickly so that the commanding officer wouldn't see it.

That night we all enjoyed the first fruit and candy we had had in months. In the following months we went on many such jaunts in Jap trucks, and usually found the guards quite lenient when away from their superiors. Often, they became very drunk, and we Americans had to drive them back in the rear of the truck.

One afternoon, while repairing roads far down on Bataan, I broke out in a profuse sweat which was accompanied by a burning fever. I struggled on the best I could for the remainder of the day and by the time we returned to camp, I felt weak, but the fever had subsided.

The next day I felt well, but the following afternoon I was afflicted with the same malady. And thus, it continued, two o'clock every other day brought on an attack of burning fever which was preceded by a bone-shaking chill. There was no doubt in my mind that I had malaria, and I could do nothing about it.

On the job, when I became too sick to work, I would ask one of the Jap overseers to feel my forehead; realizing that I was burning with fever, he would allow me to lie in the shade of the truck until it had subsided. I felt weaker by the day; but even the best of medicines would not have been of much use because we slept without mosquito nets and the locality was infested with the malaria-bearing Anopheles mosquito.

While living and working at Balanga I was introduced to the Japanese "Onsen," or bath ritual, a practice indulged in by all Jap troops regardless of station. At the end of the day a fifty-gallon oil drum was filled with fresh water and heated over an open fire. While the water was piping hot, the commanding officer of the organization enjoyed his nightly bath.

He was followed by the highest-ranking non-commissioned officer and so on down the chain of command. When the lowest ranking private finally had his turn, the water must have been quite a mess. Even under the most adverse conditions, the Jap army practiced this custom daily.

On the first of June, our guards packed all of their belongings and equipment in preparation for moving. The following day we thirty-nine remaining prisoners boarded a truck in the convoy and were told we were going to Manila. When we arrived in the city, we were taken off the truck at a vacant dance hall on Rizal Avenue, where we lived under guard for the following four days. Our hosts had taken quarters at a nearby apartment building and were enjoying an urban holiday.

Time hung rather heavily on our hands during those four days. Three times daily we were sent a bucket of rice and a pail of green soup. It had been bad enough eating that stuff when we were working, but while lying around it was pretty hard to swallow. My malaria was bothering me more than ever by now and frankly I was worried about it.

When the trucks stopped outside our quarters once more, we were glad to be leaving. We were told that our destination was a town called Culumpit, Pampanga, about sixty kilometers north of Manila.

Upon arrival at Culumpit, we disembarked at an abandoned school building that had a small, ancient Catholic church in the front yard. The area was encircled by a barbed wire fence and had sentry posts on each corner. The school was quite rundown but had a few primary readers, called "Little Verses for Little Filipinos," which provided us with hours of reading material, a blackboard on the wall, three dilapidated desks, and a toilet in the backyard.

The outhouse was partitioned off into three chambers. The door of the left compartment was marked "Boys." The door of the right compartment was marked "Girls," and the center door was boldly inscribed with "Teachers, Boys and Girls." I never did figure out that combination. When we wanted water, we were told to summon the attention of a sentry and were then to walk a block down the village street to a well, not loitering on the way.

The villagers had been forewarned about talking with us and seemed deathly frightened when we looked at them. When we approached the well, they left instantly, regardless of whether their containers had been filled or not. On my first trip to the pump, I caught sight of a Filipino girl in the window of a house directly across the road. She smiled and tried to tell me something, but I could not understand her.

When I had finished filling my canteen, she left the house and walked straight toward the well. In glancing back, I saw her place a folded piece of paper under a loose cobblestone at the base of the pump. In half an hour I returned with a five-gallon can to fill and picked up the note.

Later, back in my quarters, I read the beautiful handwriting which conveyed the following message:

"Dear Corporal Smith:

We have been warned that death is the penalty for contact with American prisoners: but if there is anything I can do to help you, it will be well worth the price. My name is —; I am twenty-four years old; and prior to the Jap occupation of Manila, I taught English at the University of the Philippines. I have never been to America but feel that I am one of you.

After the war has ended, I plan to visit the United States. We hate the Japs with all our hearts as they have pillaged our homes and killed many of our loved ones. The men in the village have organized bands that make occasional raids on the Japs. While you are in Culumpit, you will see some of their work; but no harm will come to you through the work of these guerrillas. Let me warn you against attempted escape. The Japs have placed a price of five hundred pesos on the heads of escaped Americans.

Although most of our people are loyal, there are those few who, because of starving families, would turn you in for the reward. If conditions become too bad for you to endure and escape seems your only alternative, contact me first; and I will attempt to arrange your passage on a riverboat that goes up into the Province. At any time, I can help you, I will be more than glad to do so and will do anything you ask. I will be watching through this window constantly or shall have one of the members of my family posted when you come to the well.

Your loyal pro-American friend,
(Signed) Her Name."

The note enclosed a five-peso bill. Perhaps I had better explain that "Corporal Smith" heading on her note. While repairing roads on Bataan the preceding month, I found a pair of coveralls lying by the roadside which fitted me perfectly. They had corporal's chevrons on the sleeves and the name "Smith" neatly embroidered above the left pocket.

I discarded my worn khakis and from that time on wore the coveralls constantly. As most of the men in our group were strangers to me, I was generally known as "Smith." It didn't make much difference what they called me, so I had not bothered removing the name from the garment. The morning following our arrival at Culumpit, the Jap officer in command came to our quarters and selected four of our lot.

He took us to the banks of a large river about four kilometers from our camp and produced blueprints of a proposed bridge which would span the stream. He asked if any of us had knowledge of engineering and was answered in the affirmative by a young officer who had studied civil engineering while attending West Point.

From our past experience of working for the Japs we learned that it was much to our advantage to plan a project; for when they engineered it, it was invariably wrong and made our work much more difficult. They had confidence in our ability and let us proceed with the engineering.

We asked for a boat, transit, several hundred meters of line, paper and pencil, and for the following two days we sounded various parts of the river bottom, selecting solid foundations for the pilings.

The blueprints called for a seventy-degree angle approach to the structure which would have made extremely difficult work. Through our transit readings we devised a scheme to construct a new approach by making a bend in the highway. When we submitted our proposed changes to the Jap commander, he approved, and we proceeded with the project.

We had fifty Jap soldiers and about two hundred Filipinos working on the bridge. The Filipinos were a forced labor battalion earning fifteen centavos (seven and a half cents) a day. About twenty American prisoners were working; the others were too sick to leave the billet.

I had worked on the bridge for a week when my malaria became so severe that I was forced to stay in my quarters; for as certain as the sun would rise each day, between one and three o'clock I would undergo a joint-loosening chill, followed by a high fever.

We had a mutual agreement among ourselves that when a man became sick, he moved out of the building to a grass hut across the road because many forms of disease were prevalent, and it was selfish to jeopardize the lives of others by exposing them to undiagnosed maladies. I moved my few belongings to the hut across the way and took my place with ten. other sick men lying on the floor.

During the heat of the afternoon, while undergoing a chill on that first day, I listened to one of the sick men in a delirium rambling about "Mother," "strawberry shortcake," "three no-trump," etc. The following morning, he was dead.

Before going to work each morning, a group of men came to our death house, brought us rice and soup from the Jap kitchen, cleaned the place up, wished us a speedy recovery, then went to work. Time did not permit morning burials, and by evening the corpses were in a foul condition.

At the end of my first week in the "hospital," I had seen six men join our group from across the way and had watched four men die. I felt myself become weaker by the hour and hadn't eaten a grain of rice for three days.

That afternoon a visiting Japanese doctor from Manila stopped to administer to some sick Japs and, probably as a matter of curiosity, looked in on the sick prisoners.

He spoke a little English and inquired of me, "What kind of sick you got?"

I informed him that I had malaria and possibly dysentery.

"Yes," he said, "and yellow eyes ... maybe yellow jaundice."

In reply to his interrogation regarding eating I said that I couldn't eat moldy rice.

His simple remark was, "If you do not eat rice, you will go to heaven!"

I was sick in body, but not too sick in mind to wish I could remind this doctor of the oath of Hippocrates he had taken upon his graduation from medical school; something about administering to and relieving the suffering of all men, regardless of race, color, or creed. His glittering saber checked my tongue, however, and with his last encouraging remark about going to heaven, he departed.

The next morning when the clean-up party entered the shack, I felt too weak and too discouraged to even move.

A foot pressed against my side, and I heard a voice saying, "We'll have to dig a long grave for Reynolds tonight."

This remark frightened me, so I assured them that I was not dead and that they would not be digging a grave for me; however, I had heard other men make the same statement and die three hours later. When the men left, I resolved to make one last stand for my life. I washed up as best I could with the water that was left in my canteen; then I made my way to the road and proceeded to walk toward the village. It was a strenuous effort reaching the pump and I was forced to rest before returning.

While sitting at the well, I caught the eye of the Filipino girl across the street and she motioned for me to remain where I was. In a few minutes, her little brother came to the pump to fill a pitcher and dropped a note at my feet without saying a word. I returned to my quarters to read the illicit message.

She wrote that she knew I was sick because I hadn't been to the well for days and that I looked terribly thin. If I would return to the well in an hour, leaving a note describing the nature of my illness, she would go to Manila and try to get medicine for me. With shaky handwriting I scribbled out the requested information.

For the remainder of the day I stayed on my feet as much as possible, having seen too many examples of what happens to men who lie down. That night I went to the town pump once more, and the girl left her house carrying a large water bucket.

She calmly smiled, produced a package from the bucket, handed it to me, and then proceeded to fill the container with water. I was amazed at her boldness and realized she had been sincere when in her first note she said she would do anything to help me. I concealed the package in my coveralls as much as possible and under the cover of approaching darkness, managed to pass the guards without their seeing the protruding front of my clothes.

The package contained a bottle of quinine for malaria, a box of sulfathiazole tablets for dysentery, a bowl of custard, a couple of pounds of sugar, and two cans of sweetened condensed milk. I knew then that my life had been saved!

By taking the medicine according to the instructions on the labels and eating my rice by camouflaging it with condensed milk or sugar, I gained strength daily and was soon in a position to help some of my less fortunate friends.

When my medicine supply was exhausted, the girl at the pump instructed me in the native method of extracting quinine from the bark of the cinchona tree. The bark is boiled for many hours and exudes a yellow syrup-like juice, very bitter in taste but highly effective in the curing of malaria. I used large quantities of the bark, spending several hours daily boiling down the syrup and bottling it. Not only was it effective in its curative powers but was also a fine prophylaxis against malaria. I don't know where the bark came from, but two nights weekly I found a bundle of it lying beside the well and carried it back to our quarters in the guise of kindling.

Our newly-acquired source of quinine abruptly halted the deaths from malaria, but yellow jaundice and dysentery were still claiming the lives of many men.

I thought I had fully recovered from my illness when one night a fire blazed into the sky from one of the Jap buildings.

We all rushed to the scene in fear that our quarters might be destroyed if the fire spread, but in attempting to run, I fell flat on my face in the gravel. My legs were too weak to run or climb stairs. I later learned that the fire was the work of Filipino guerrillas because the building was a gasoline and oil storehouse.

I did not return to work on the bridge but stayed around the quarters gaining strength and helping the other sick men as much as possible. One morning while washing at the well, a strange Filipino dropped a note at my feet in passing; a note which suggested that I visit a certain home in the village that evening. The house proved to be that of a high government official in the Province. Shortly after nightfall a companion and I stealthily advanced down the village street to the archway of the home of our host.

Just before reaching it a blinding flash of lightning made the area bright as day. We were plainly visible to any Jap within three blocks. It was spooky, to say the least, knowing there was a price on our heads; but hungry men will take such chances. When we reached the gate, a Filipino stepped from behind a tree and told us to enter through a trap door in the kitchen of the house, stating that he would stand guard at the gate until we returned.

All was in readiness when we arrived. Eight women and several men were in the kitchen, and there was an abundance of food, excellently prepared, including rice, of course, pork, turkey, and fish.

My partner and I were seated at a large table and proceeded to eat our fill of the first meat we had had in months. During the meal, strange noises came from the front of the house and the men and women talked excitedly with one another in Tagalog (Ta'gaw log), the Philippine language. I inquired about their anxiety and was told that several Jap officers were being entertained in the living room.

As the meal progressed, I became more and more uneasy, for the men seemed to be arguing among themselves. My buddy and I exchanged knowing looks, and I confided to him that I suspected we were being "sold out."

I whispered to him, "In a minute I am going to smash the kerosene lamp on the table. When I do, you dive for the trap door, and I will be right behind you."

As I feigned reaching for a plate of rice in order to extinguish the light, the door from the living room opened and the girl who had provided me with food and medicine appeared.

My fears were calmed by her presence because I felt certain she would not be involved in such a traitorous scheme. Needless to say, we finished our meal quickly, thanked our hosts, and departed with a neatly bound package of food for some of the fellows back in camp.

However, again when we approached the archway in front of the house, an arm grabbed us from behind a tree and a voice whispered, "Don't move. There are Japs ten feet from you!"

We froze in our tracks until the voices of the passing Japs died out, thanked our Filipino guard, and then, to the accompaniment of all of the barking dogs in the village, returned to camp by following the river. We hadn't been missed during our hour of absence, but it was one of the longest and most thrilling hours in my life.

One afternoon, a truckload of forty men arrived from Cabanatuan to re-enforce our detail. I knew two of the men in the group and immediately inquired about conditions in the central camp. I learned that thousands of men had died and were still perishing in alarming numbers. Then I realized that I was better off being away from the main body of prisoners, for help such as I had obtained in the village would have been impossible in a camp of thousands of men.

During those days the Japs permitted us to read their newspapers, such as Manila Tribune and Tokyo Times, which were printed in English. The papers were filled largely with propaganda and literature urging closer unity between Filipinos and Japanese.

"The Filipinos," the newspapers claimed, "are Orientals, therefore brothers of the Japanese. Although they have been exploited by Americans for years, there is no reason why they should not now live in close harmony with their liberators under the Greater East Asia Co-prosperity Sphere."

Their propaganda was persuasive but the actions of their army of occupation were not conducive to tranquility. In every village throughout the Commonwealth, the army maintained guard stations on the main street. Passing villagers were required to remove their headgear and bow deeply to the six soldiers who remained seated. When riding on a bicycle or a horse-drawn vehicle, they were forced to dismount and bow.

One Sunday morning the bells of the village church were tolling and the populace of Culumpit was wending its way to the chapel, everyone pausing momentarily at the sentry station to pay his respects to the Emperor.

A young Filipino and his wife walked leisurely down the street, hands clasped, with prayer books under their arms. The woman was noticeably pregnant.

When they bowed at the guard shack and proceeded on their way, the guards shouted for them to stop, then all six left their seats to make fun of the expectant mother.

They pointed at her, laughing loudly. All the while the young husband burned with rage. The muscles under his silk shirt bulged and he clenched his fists in attempted self-control, while his wife pleaded with him to hold his temper, knowing too well what would happen if he gave vent to his desire to crush one of their heads.

Is there any wonder why Japs who ventured into the villages at night alone were often found the following morning with their heads neatly severed by a native's bolo?

The ravages of malnutrition manifested themselves in the form of scurvy and pellagra, which caused large areas of skinned patches on men's hands. Their tongues became so painfully swelled that the victims couldn't talk, and minor wounds caused by splinters or scratches developed into major infections.

In addition to the annoying results of malnutrition, we were troubled with the ever-present tropical fungus irritations similar to athlete's foot. In an effort to check the malignant growth, I had obtained a small bottle of alcohol which I used to sponge the blisters after piercing them with a needle.

One afternoon, while administering this treatment to the soles of my feet, a Jap sentry, obviously drunk, entered the shack and immediately noticed what I was doing. He removed the bayonet from his rifle and proceeded to operate on my foot.

Of course, I objected; but when I grasped his hand in an effort to stop him, I realized that he meant business for he threatened to stab me with the instrument.

Much to my discomfort, he dug out the base of each blister with the point of his bayonet and left my foot practically in ribbons and covered with blood. I cleaned up the mess and stopped the bleeding with alcohol but was forced to hobble around on the heel of the foot for the next week. However, he might have known what he was doing for the infection never returned.

By this time, we realized that the Japs were making no attempt to learn English and we were beginning to pick up some of the words in their language. Most of us now knew the commands for work, stop, rest, eat, come here, as well as hello, goodbye, and knew how to count and to tell time in Japanese.

Due to our late arrival in the Philippines prior to the war, I had had little opportunity to observe the Filipino mode of life as a free man. However, while living in various villages during my captivity, I made illicit visits to many native homes and was amused by their strange customs.

All homes in the Philippine Islands are made of bamboo with grass roofs and are perched on wooden stilts about six feet above the ground. These stilts serve several purposes, such as the elimination of plumbing, since wide spaces between the strips composing the floor in the homes serve in lieu of toilets.

The ever-present hogs under the house function as disposal plants as well as being the family's meat supply. Perhaps the primary function of the poles, however, is to keep the house dry during the rainy season when several feet of water often cover the ground. In a large percentage of native homes, which are practically devoid of furniture, one finds a Singer sewing machine in the living room; consequently, both sexes of Filipinos are adept tailors capable of converting a bed sheet into several fancy sport shirts in a short time.

Many of the younger residents of Manila dress in immaculate whites and idle away their time on the street corners. The majority of these men are graduates of the University of the Philippines, many of whom hold law degrees from that institution. Having become accustomed to the leisure of the metropolis, they refuse to return to the humble provincial farms of their parents whose hard-earned pesos made possible their education.

Women of the Philippines wear a puffed-shouldered dress while the men are invariably clad in the traditional sport slacks and "Barong Tagalog," a sport shirt with exposed tails. This custom of dress originated in the Islands during the days of Spanish reign when a decree was issued ordering shirt tails exhibited to prove the Filipino's acceptance of the white man's use of toilet paper instead of shirt tails.

The diet of our little brown brothers is relatively simple, consisting largely of rice supplemented by meat, fish, and vegetables. Of course, they have their peculiar national dishes, one of the favorites being the "baloot," or unhatched chicken, hard-boiled in the shell. This delicacy is sold by vendors in Manila and throughout the commonwealth as ice cream is sold in America. Since the arrival of the white man in the Philippines and his introduction of Occidental food, the stature of the Filipino has increased five inches and his longevity increased by fifteen years.

With the last group of men sent from the central camp as re-enforcements to the detail was a strange, suspicious-looking individual who talked with no one. He was reluctant to disclose his identity, but I finally gained a little information from him. He was a German-Jew refugee who had arrived in Manila shortly before the war and had been conscripted into the Philippine Army upon the commencement of hostilities.

For several weeks, this fellow acted strangely and seemed to be carrying on a correspondence with someone through notes given to certain Filipinos working at the bridge. One evening at roll call we were short one man and it was he. The Japs didn't act unduly alarmed but conducted a thorough search of the village. Ten armed guards each took five prisoners with lanterns and visited every house in the area. It was late at night, and the Filipinos were frightened at being awakened at such an hour. The Japs were very loud, hammering on the doors of the huts and shouting roughly in Japanese.

We acted as interpreters, calming the frightened child-like natives as follows: "Don't be frightened. One of our men has escaped and we are going to search your house. If you have seen this man, please tell us, for we must find him."

By three o'clock in the morning the search had proven futile and we returned to our quarters.

The following day the men went to work as usual, and nothing seemed to have happened. After supper that night, we were ordered to assemble in a tennis court across the road from the billet, where a Japanese officer addressed us in very poor English with the following speech, "Because one of your number has escaped, five men must be punished. When I call your names, you will step forward to be shot!"

And so, he called, at random and very slowly, the names of five men, giving each man in the group ample opportunity to die a thousand deaths before the next one was read off. When each of the five men heard his summons, he stepped smartly from ranks and stood at attention before the Jap officer. Not a whimper was heard from any of them and when they were ordered to mount the awaiting trucks, they called farewells to their comrades. One unfortunate man called to his brother, "Tell Mom what happened."

On the truck which took the doomed men to their execution was a fifteen-man firing squad, dressed immaculately in full uniform and white gloves. Each of the condemned men was given a pick and shovel as he mounted the vehicle, and the American officer in our group was forced to go along as a witness.

While the five men were being taken on their death ride, the remainder of us were forced to remain on the tennis court under guard and were reminded that if one of the adjudged men should escape before his execution, five more of us would be shot. They were driven three kilometers away.

In the pouring rain two hours later, the American officer returned with a grim story. The men had been forced to dig their own shallow graves; each was given a cigarette and then ordered to kneel in his grave.

All of them refused blindfolds. In shaking hands with the officer, one man handed him a baby shoe which he had been carrying, saying, "I guess I won't need this anymore."

Another was missed completely by the firing squad and calmly announced that they had better try again. They did, this time riddling him with bullets. A Jap officer administered a mercy shot to each man's head with an automatic pistol, and the witness was ordered to fill the graves with dirt. They had died like real soldiers and true Americans. Because of the brave actions of these five men, we gained untold respect from the Japanese.

Near the end of August, the bridge upon which we had been working was completed. A dedication ceremony was planned for the following Saturday when a Jap engineering officer from Manila would arrive to see the newly-completed project. Great plans were laid for the celebration as the Japs had purchased and commandeered hogs, chickens and goats, and had prepared for a tremendous feast.

When a truckload of beer arrived, everything was set for the gala occasion. During the ceremony and accompanying feast, we prisoners watched from our billet without being given an additional grain of rice.

Later in the day, one of the Empire Builders must have discovered an excess of beer and sent over one bottle for every two men. While watching the gluttons voraciously stuffing themselves with food and liquor, we were disgusted but did enjoy a good laugh during the bridge dedication.

As the visiting officer, riding in an expensive American touring car, crossed the span, he was followed by a garrison of Japs, marching to the music of the local Filipino brass band which was loudly playing "God Bless America!"

The bystanders from the village cheered wildly, glancing knowingly at us; the Japs were none the wiser. The following day we boarded trucks and were sent to the Philippine Military Prison Camp No. 1 at Cabanatuan. It was September 2, 1942.

6 - CABANATUAN

UPON ARRIVAL AT THE MAIN CAMP, we were searched as a matter of routine and were then turned loose in the compound. American authorities, dressed in ragged clothing, assigned us to "barracks" which proved to be grass shacks where ninety men slept shoulder to shoulder on bays, or long shelves which ran the length of the building in two tiers.

Many of my old friends from the squadron were there, and many of them were not. It was shocking to learn that so many of the fellows had died. We sat up quite late that first night smoking the cigarettes I had brought with me, a very scarce item in the main camp.

The following morning at five o'clock we were roused and had our morning *bango*, or roll call. Four Jap guards made a tour of the camp, checking the number of men standing in formation before each building.

All of the prisoners were arranged in squads of ten. Should one man escape, the other nine of his squad would be shot. Upon assignment to such a group I immediately told the other members that, if they were entertaining any ideas of escape, to let me know and I would go with them. At least a man had a chance in attempting escape, but none whatever by staying behind and facing a Jap rifle squad.

After a meager breakfast of rice and water, called "soup," we were assigned our duties for the day, duties such as fence repairing, latrine digging, gravel hauling, wood cutting, and burial detail. The names of twenty men were called for the burial party, which at first amazed me; but I reasoned that each barracks must take its turn furnishing the burial party.

When informed that each building provided that number of men daily, I immediately inquired as to the number of men dying each day, and was told that the average was between forty-five and fifty. My brain began spinning with figures; three thousand men in camp and with that number dying daily, I would live until Thanksgiving at the longest, even if I were the last man to die!

So large a number of men was required to bury our less fortunate comrades because the corpses had to be carried four kilometers; and since all of us were in a weakened condition it required four men to bear each litter. The graves were nothing more than huge pits about the size of a house foundation excavation and only a few feet in depth.

These burial pits were dug each day for the following day's burial. When it rained during the night, the pits would fill with water, but nothing could be done about it. The corpses must be buried either in water-filled graves or dry ones. Several crosses, mounted on each burial plot, bore the names of the men entombed there.

At the conclusion of such burial parties, we removed our hats and listened to a few words of prayer said for our departed comrades. While we gathered around the covered grave and bowed our heads, this moment was invariably desecrated by the Jap guards who chose it as the time to urinate, thus expressing their contempt for Christianity. In advanced cases, cerebral malaria manifests itself in the form of a coma so death-like that a stethoscope is required to ascertain the languid heartbeat.

One cold, rainy day we dumped our defunct cargo into a water-filled pit, as usual, when an observant chaplain detected a stream of bubbles coming from the nose of one body. In spite of the protests from the Jap guards, the naked body was carried back to camp in the pouring rain, and the man was revived by the rectal administration of liquid quinine.

Last Christmas, I received a greeting card from this man whom we almost buried alive and who was reclaimed from death at Cabanatuan. Often the driving torrents of rain washed away the earth covering the graves during the night and the following day the burial detail found arms and legs protruding from them. The dirt in the burial lot had assumed a dark red hue from the blood of thousands of men buried in the mud just a few inches below the surface.

In addition to the elements, wild dogs wrought great havoc upon the bodies laid to rest. These untamed beasts tunneled into the center of the graves and feasted on the bodies of our dead. On moonlit nights we often heard the baying dogs in the cemetery, knowing that they were eating the bodies of our friends.

During September, one man escaped and the remaining nine of his group were promptly shot. On another occasion three men bribed a Jap sentry at the fence to let them slip out to a nearby village in search of food. When they returned with a sack of groceries, the sentry had been relieved, and his successor caught them attempting to re-enter the camp.

For two days, as an example to others who might have similar ideas, they were tied to stakes in the scorching sun and signs announcing their impending execution were hung from their necks. The American officer in charge of the camp had a heated argument with the Japanese camp commander. He drew the Jap's attention to the fact that, in International Law governing prisoners of war, there is no clause sanctioning the execution of prisoners for leaving and attempting to re-enter a prison camp. However, the Jap, not to be outwitted, produced a book of American army regulations and opened it to a chapter authorizing the execution of any soldier caught looting during time of war.

"Those men were looting," he said, "and what is law in your army will hold in this camp, too!"

The following day the thirst-craved men requested that they be shot without further delay. They were; after they had dug their own graves. The alarming death rate continued for weeks.

One night early in October, we were ordered to assemble at one end of the camp where a large platform had been erected. We stood around the structure, wondering what was going to take place and watching the sky overhead, for a blue moon was shining. Several cumulus clouds in the sky and some unusual meteorological phenomena must have accounted for the vivid color of the moon. A Jap officer, accompanied by a staff of four, mounted the stand. An interpreter announced that the commanding officer was going to deliver a speech, and that he would interpret it for us. The commander began, spoke a sentence or two, paused and waited for the translation into English and then continued.

In a high-pitched voice, the interpreter, holding a kerosene lantern, announced, "The commanding offisah he say today you are war prisoner! No more captive, now prisoner of war. You escape, you be catched and shoot!"

We were laboring under the apprehension that we had been prisoners of war for months, but obviously had not been considered so by the Japanese. At any rate, after this date of being officially recognized as prisoners, our food ration was improved, and meat became a part of our diet.

A small quantity of sugar was also included in our rations, and each week four carabao (water buffalo) were butchered in the camp. Everyone who worked was paid at the rate of fifteen centavos (seven and one-half cents) per day which could be used to purchase bananas, coconuts and tobacco from the Japanese. As the result of the increase in rations, our death rate dropped considerably, and on some days, we buried as few as four men.

In our group of prisoners, we had doctors and chaplains. The doctors' hands were tied by the lack of medicine or equipment with which to work, but the chaplains carried on with their work through the most adverse conditions. Besides conducting simple memorial services for the dead and comforting the sick, they had been permitted to conduct religious services for all denominations once a week since our recognition as prisoners of war. That day, Sunday, was a day of rest for the entire camp.

With the reverse side of milk can labels used as hymnals and the congregation sitting on the ground before an altar converted from a barrel, the religious services were simple. I remembered something from my childhood about, "Where two or more are gathered together in my name, there am I in the midst of them..."

Crude as these services were, the true spirit in which they were conducted prevailed, and they were a great source of encouragement in days that seemed too dark to endure.

During those days, an acute water shortage existed in Cabanatuan. Two one-inch pipes served the entire group, and cooking rice and soup required large quantities of water. Practically the entire camp took advantage of the rainstorms in which to bathe. Due to a diet composed mostly of liquids and to our sleeping on rough bamboo slats, we made frequent trips to the urinal at night. Even at 2 A.M. we often stood in line at a water faucet waiting to fill our canteens.

Two days before Christmas of 1942, Red Cross packages arrived in the village station and were transported to the camp in carabao carts for distribution on Christmas day. Each man was given an eleven-pound box containing corned beef, cheese, crackers, chocolate and cigarettes. No wonder morale was high that day and the burial detail had to bury but one corpse; that of a malnourished fellow who attempted to consume his entire eleven pounds of food at one time.

On January 3, 1943, I was detailed to leave Cabanatuan with a hundred and fifty other men on a labor detail. We did not know where we were going, but then it didn't make much difference. Just before leaving camp I was given a card to send home.

There was little I could say except to fill in the few blanks on the card that looked something like this:

JAPANESE IMPERIAL ARMY
I am interned at. . . . .
My health is. . . . .
Give my best regards to. . .
Your loving . . . .
e - e - - - - - e. e. - e - e. e. e.

The card did bear my signature, however, and, when delivered to my parents eight months later, was the first word that told them I had survived the Bataan campaign and Death March.

7 - LIPA, BATANGAS

WE LEFT CAMP THE FOLLOWING morning at three o'clock, each man carrying a rice ball in his pocket for his mid-day meal. After walking ten kilometers to a railway depot, we were crowded into two boxcars where we spent the next eight hours en route to Manila. After changing trains and stretching our legs in Manila, we arrived late at night in Lipa in the province of Batangas. We were greeted at the new camp by two hundred other prisoners, several of whom I had known on Bataan. They described the nature of the work they were performing, and it sounded rather strenuous.

Constructing an airstrip on the site of a coconut grove was not too inviting. Each tree was about forty feet in height and three feet in diameter at its base. These were planted in rows twenty feet apart extending five miles. The trees were chopped down and dragged away; then the roots were extracted with picks and shovels to facilitate leveling the ground for a runway.

We were informed that, although the work was hard, the food was correspondingly fair. Meat was served once each day, giving each man about two ounces. Rice was plentiful, and sugar was issued to the camp at the rate of ten pounds a day. We also learned that the rate of pay was the same as in the central camp, and we would have buying privileges.

The best news of all was that, during the four months the original detail had been stationed at Lipa, not one man had died. Our meals proved to be nothing but rice and soup. When meat was issued it was put into the soup. The same was true of vegetables, fish and sugar. When the Jap in charge of our supplies brought the articles of issue into the kitchen, he tossed the unwashed vegetables, uncleaned fish, and a sack of sugar into the boiling soup cauldron.

The resulting combination was not very appetizing; one can imagine the taste of sweet fish soup. However, we did manage to eat the stuff and derived energy from it. In Japan prior to the war, sugar was a rare delicacy; consequently, when Jap soldiers were in a position to obtain unlimited quantities of it, they abused its use horribly, using it in every form of cooking.

I once witnessed a Japanese mess sergeant open a case of a well-known American brand of pork and beans, thoroughly wash off the tomato sauce, cover the washed beans with a vast quantity of sugar, and boil them for three hours.

Work on the field progressed in routine until a truck drove into the compound one day and an elderly, ragged American officer carrying an old barracks bag stepped down.

Several of the fellows recognized the man as a Catholic chaplain they had not seen or heard of since the march from Bataan. His story was most interesting. On the Death March from Bataan he had fallen by the wayside in a malarial coma and was mistaken for dead by the Japs. After the procession had passed, friendly Filipinos in a nearby village found him and nursed him back to health in their homes.

After his recovery, he organized a guerrilla band which terrorized the Japs on Luzon for seven months. During his reign as guerrilla chief, he was in radio contact with MacArthur's forces in Australia; consequently, he had a great deal of war news to relate to us. Two months prior to his arrival at Lipa, he had surrendered to the Japanese in the mountainous regions of Northern Luzon. The reason for his surrendering he never related and never will because the ship on which he was later sent to Japan was sunk by Allied submarines.

He had been sent to Lipa to fill the position of chaplain and did a splendid job, raising the morale of the men when they were discouraged, and visiting with us while we worked on the airstrip.

Occasionally he took off his shirt and swung a pick for a half hour in order to give a tired man a rest. Three days a week he conducted religious services in camp. Twice on Sunday he held Catholic mass and once a week Protestant worship; on Saturday he officiated at Jewish rites for the handful of Jews in our lot. These religious ceremonies, of course, were not permitted to interfere with work on the airstrip and thus were held either early in the morning or late at night.

During my months of living and working with the Japanese, I concluded that the yellow race was never meant to be in authority. Even while we were the slaves of this egotistical race, they often seemed to feel inferior to us. When an engineering problem arose or when a piece of machinery failed to function, they invariably turned to us for assistance.

One afternoon a Jap guard slipped under the dual rear wheels of a moving truck which crushed part of his chest and one shoulder. His fellow soldiers grew panicky, shaking the man and calling him by name.

Two of our men, taking command of the situation, ordered the Japs to prepare a stretcher on the floor of an empty truck where they gently laid the injured man and then drove to a hospital in the nearby village without the accompaniment of guards. An hour later, when the men returned with the truck, the Japs had regained their self-composure and were very indignant over their not having been consulted with regard to the moving of the victim to the hospital.

Perhaps to the reader such an act of caring for an injured Jap sounds strange; however, deep-rooted in every American is a keen reluctance to see anyone suffer, regardless of race or color. We could not look at a suffering Jap and laugh. Time after time, when a situation arose which called for fast, cool thinking, the Japs were "caught with their kimonos down," and they turned to us with a bewildered look as much as to say, "What is the thing for us to do now?"

While working on the airstrip, as usual, a new Jap driver appeared on the scene one day, hauling gravel with his truck.

While we were loading his vehicle, two of the men with whom I was working were carrying on a conversation in Spanish. When we had completed our loading, instead of driving off with his load, the driver smiled and in Castilian Spanish spoke to the two. Through their interpretation, we learned that the young Jap had lived in Peru for fifteen years. Just prior to the outbreak of the international chaos, he had been ordered to return to his native land; Japan, but had replied that his mining interests in Peru would not warrant his leaving.

The retort from the Jap authorities informed him that, should he fail to return in ninety days, his parents, still residing in Japan, would be killed.

I believe he told the truth because he did not mingle with the other Jap soldiers except as his work demanded and appeared to be an outcast in their midst.

Work offered little diversion for the following four months; however, my eyes were troubling me a great deal. At first, they were extremely sensitive to artificial light. In the center of the building in which we were housed was a ten-watt lightbulb. After dark I could not even stand in a far corner of the room with the light, so I usually sat outside until "lights out," or went to bed, covering my head with a blanket.

Soon they reached the stage where any source of light caused them to burn and water, and there was nothing I could do but avoid the light as much as possible, keeping my eyes to the ground while at work and while en route to and from the field. I was certain that there were splinters of steel in each eye, and repeatedly asked fellows to see if they could remove them, but they could find nothing wrong.

When a visiting Jap doctor stopped at the camp one day, I asked permission to see him. He examined my eyes, said there was nothing he could do for me, but assured me that my working days were over.

The next morning when a truck left for Manila, I, with my few belongings, was aboard. The scenery of Southern Batangas is beautiful; but because of the light and wind, I had a rag tied over my eyes attempting to alleviate the smarting, so I cannot describe any of it.

8 - BILIBID PRISON

I HAD WORKED FOR TWENTY-NINE days of the previous month and had wages due me in the amount of four pesos and thirty centavos ($2.15). However, because I hadn't completed the entire work-month, I was not paid. Upon arrival at Manila I was taken to Bilibid Prison in the heart of the city. Formerly it was the federal prison of the Philippines, having come into existence during the days of the Spanish regime in the islands.

The prison was surrounded by twenty-foot stone walls with sentry stations atop the walls at fifty-foot intervals and had a 30,000-volt wire topping the stockade. The buildings were in a decrepit state, not having been used for twenty years prior to the Jap occupation of the islands, but provided a safe-keeping place for American prisoners. Inside the walls, the prison was under the jurisdiction of American Navy Prisoner Personnel; that is to say, the Japanese maintained an office in the forepart of the prison but, with the exception of several roving sentries inside the perimeter, the administration was in the hands of American authorities.

Although the prison was called a military prison hospital, there was little the doctors could do for the men with the shortage of medicine and equipment. The Japs furnished aspirin in minute quantities; equipment was practically nil. A doctor once confided in me that his only piece of equipment was a New Testament. Invariably when a sick man came to him for treatment, the doctor administered two aspirin tablets and read a chapter from the Testament to the man.

Upon arrival, I was asked my ailment, and then assigned to a building in which I was to sleep. It turned out to be the execution chamber of the prison with the base of the electric chair still cemented to the floor. Signs on the walls announced in three languages, "DANGER—HIGH VOLTAGE. WEAR RUBBER GLOVES WHEN HANDLING THIS SWITCH."

A doctor diagnosed my ailment as corneal ulcers, and said there was nothing he could do except retard the malignant growth by keeping my eyes in a constant state of dilation.

For two months my eyes were kept in this condition. I was assured that the growth would not advance, but without the needed vitamins their condition would not improve. As I could stand no light, I was forced to lie on a wooden cot with a rag tightly bound over my eyes. Several men who had the same affliction in an advanced state had lost the sight of one eye completely because the milky-white growth had enveloped the eyeball, leaving a repulsive dead-white film over the entire surface. Those two months were horribly long. The days were hot and sticky, and there was nothing to do but lie there, swatting at unseen flies and thinking of home. In addition to flies and mosquitoes, our quarters were infested with bedbugs.

Many of the fellows in my building were bed-ridden, encased in huge plaster casts as the result of war injuries or accidents which occurred while working for the Japs. The bed-bugs lived by the thousands under those filthy casts, and nearly drove the poor boys crazy. During that time, I re-lived my entire life; thinking of everything I had ever done. Someone would tell me that it was Sunday or Monday, and I would figure the difference in time zones between Manila and my home in Duluth, and then wonder what my parents were doing at that time.

I could picture them in the family pew at church and wished desperately that I could be there with them. A man deprived of his eyesight learns to do lots of thinking ... and praying. At the end of those dreary months, word was received that Red Cross supplies had arrived at the pier and would be distributed in the camps soon. When they arrived in Bilibid, we found that, in addition to food packages, a supply of medicines and vitamins was included. My doctor placed me on a priority vitamin list immediately, and the following day I was subjected to a course of injections and pills.

Twice daily at 8 A.M. and 1 P.M., I was given a shot in the arm and a handful of the precious tablets and capsules.

At the end of two weeks I felt an improvement, and after a month of the treatment, felt certain that my eyes were being benefited.

This course of super-vitamins was administered to me for three months, at which time an eye examination revealed that the ulcers had disappeared and only their scars remained. I was taken off the routine for the benefit of men who also needed the same course of injections badly.

For the following seven months I stayed in Bilibid resting my eyes, with occasional examinations to make certain that the ulcers had not returned. That year spent in the prison hospital provided the most pleasant memories I have of prison life. We had no work to do; thus, our time was our own. I made many acquaintances, some of them most unusual.

When the Japs took the Philippines, there were many American and European civilians from all walks of life living in the islands; missionaries, beachcombers, doctors, gamblers, teachers, con-men, professional fighters, and soldiers of fortune. Each of these men had a fascinating story to tell.

One day while idling away the afternoon, someone produced a deck of wilted cards and proposed a session of bridge. Lacking a partner, I invited a white-haired stranger to make up the fourth hand. He accepted the invitation and played a most brilliant game of bridge.

At the end of the game (my partner saw to it that we won by a tremendous margin), our guest proceeded to tell each man what system of bridge he played, whether Culbertson, Fry, Foster, or Irvin. I, it seemed, played such an unorthodox game that it could not be diagnosed. To demonstrate his uncanny ability of remembering cards which had been played, he asked one of us to lay a half deck of cards face up one at a time.

When this was finished, he named each card that had been played and then called the names of the cards left in the unused portion of the deck. We had to be very cautious when inviting strangers to a game of cards, especially when stakes were involved.

Upon inquiring among the older residents of Manila, I learned that our white-haired friend was one of the biggest gambling house operators in the Orient prior to the fall of the Philippines, and had often been the guest of Manuel Quezon on board the latter's yacht, The Casiana, scene of many of the world's largest poker games.

Conversation was perhaps our most frequently-indulged-in pastime. Every man in the camp was an adventurer of some sort, and we comprised a very cosmopolitan group. Many of the characters were fugitives from justice, and had been residing in the Orient under the protection of non-extradition laws. A handsome, middle-aged man who slept next to me related some experiences that would make a fascinating book. The man, whom I shall refer to as Mr. X, had the bluest eyes I have ever seen.

Having been born of American parents into a life of adventure in the Malay states, he had spent his entire life roaming around the world in quest of fortune, adventure, and the woman of his dreams whom he had yet to meet. During his travels, he had fought in five wars, learned to speak four languages, and amassed a sizable fortune.

A number of years ago, Mr. X and a group of confederates were active in the revolution and overthrow of a small South American government. When the existing machine had been ousted, Mr. X and his party of rogues established themselves as officials of the country just long enough to lay their hands on the treasury. The small craft in which they attempted to escape with the treasure was shipwrecked. The narrator of the story still knew the exact location of the loot and planned to finance an expedition to the site upon his liberation; but, unfortunately, he died of a heart attack a year before MacArthur's return to the Philippines.

Food was a matter of primary importance to the inmates of Bilibid because we were constantly hungry. One day when a Jap truck driver with a burlap sack containing something alive approached me, I was interested, especially upon learning that the bag contained a large white duck which he offered to sell me for forty dollars.

Having experienced some good luck in a poker game the day before, I was in fair financial condition, and purchased the fowl, but found him to be very thin. Having seen Filipinos force-feed poultry, I decided to try their method. I fastened the duck to a plank with small tacks through the webbed portions of its feet to keep it from exercising. From the same Jap truck driver, I purchased a bushel of seed-corn which I boiled into a mush for the bird. Twelve times daily, I fed my duck by forcing large quantities of the corn down its throat with a stick covered with a cloth, always keeping a vessel of water in front of him from which he drank about a quart a day.

When the bushel of corn was gone, my bird was so fat that he couldn't have walked had I released him. Needless to say, three buddies and I had a wonderful feast on Thanksgiving Day, 1943!

As my birthday approached in December, it looked like another anniversary without even a cake, and I vowed to do something about it.

From an acquaintance I purchased two cups of uncooked rice, which I ground into flour, using a bottle as a rolling pin. For a leavening agent, I made a sourdough composed of cooked rice-paste and sugar, which I allowed to ferment for several days. A melted chocolate bar hoarded from a Red Cross package provided the frosting; and on the night of December 14, a couple of friends and I celebrated my twenty-fourth birthday in a manner I would have enjoyed having my parents look in on. In January, the Japs interviewed each Air Corps man in the prison in an effort to find various types of aircraft specialists, such as instrument specialists, propeller experts, bombsight maintenance men and the like, who could be advantageously employed in the Imperial Japanese Air Force.

The consultation began in alphabetical order; consequently, my name was far down the list. When at last I was summoned to the Japanese office, an elderly interpreter spread my military record on the desk before him and attempted to strike up a friendly conversation as follows, "From Minnesota, eh? Mighty cold up there. Spent twenty-five years in Utah myself, and that was cold enough. Now then, Sergeant Reynolds, I see by your record that you are a college man; an aeronautical engineer, no doubt. Just what were your duties in the Air Corps?"

I replied that in school I had majored in English and psychology, and that my Air Corps job was that of a file clerk and office janitor.

The interpreter shouted in disgust, "And you were promoted to a non-commissioned officer in so short a time because you scrubbed the office so well, I suppose! You are the one hundred and seventieth man I have interviewed, and thus far I have found a hundred and thirteen cooks, forty-nine latrine orderlies, and eight clerks. Just who in your organization was responsible for keeping your planes in the air?"

With that he dismissed me. Needless to say, they found no aeronautical specialists in our lot. Sometime later, we were given forms to complete stating our civilian occupations. Machinists, tool and die makers, and other specialists would undoubtedly have been sent to Japan to aid in the country's war industry. Before the completed forms were returned to the Japs, I had the opportunity of reading several hundred of them, and found the majority of occupations listed as ballet dancers, hairdressers, piano tuners, shoe salesmen, and figure skaters.

What a worthless group of Americans we must have seemed to the Japs! One night the Japs announced that they were going to show us a movie in the courtyard of the prison. All of the men in the compound turned out for the event, many of them on crutches or walking with crude artificial limbs. The picture proved to be an American film that had been in Manila for years. It must have been patched and repaired a thousand times, but we enjoyed what we saw of it, especially the music!

When the picture was half finished, a scream pierced the air from the rear of the outdoor amphitheater and a sudden stampede came thundering toward the screen. I, because of faulty vision, was sitting near the screen, and suddenly found myself being trampled upon by hordes of panic-stricken men.

I picked myself up and surged with the crowd as far as the screen, which had been hung on a stone wall, and could go no further.

Someone shouted for silence, and then ordered every man back to his respective building. The Japs came around, locked all the doors and windows and proceeded to count the men in each building. It was not until morning that I learned what had happened.

During the movie, two men had decided it was an ideal time to escape, and sneaked to the fore portion of the compound. They scaled the wall; then with the aid of a two-by-four, one held the hot wire up while the other crawled under it. The first man succeeded, but his partner touched the 30,000-volt wire, causing an alarm to sound in the Japanese guardhouse. The guards rushed to the scene.

Meanwhile, the movie continued; all of us oblivious to what was going on. The Japs cut the current, dragged the stunned man down, and then rushed outside of the prison walls to apprehend the man who had made good his escape. They found a Filipino who was mistaken for the fugitive, lurking in the shadows, and promptly bayoneted him. When the guards returned to the compound, they were dragging the unconscious man by the hair and blood was dripping from one of the Japs' bayonets.

The scene naturally frightened the men in the rear of the movie audience, and they began their mad dash forward. Things tightened down considerably after the escape, but no one was shot. The unfortunate partner of the man who made good his escape recovered from his electrical shock, and for five days was questioned in an attempt to ascertain the whereabouts of his more successful companion. During that five-day period, he was fed nothing, and the Japs' questioning must have proven futile because he was taken to Fort Santiago to stand trial for his life.

The name "Santiago" held a note of terror for all of the prisoners, for its infamous reputation had spread to every camp in the islands. Built by the Spanish prior to the insurrection, it was a sixteenth-century masterpiece in the study of human torture. Special cells measuring three feet in height and breadth had been constructed, and men imprisoned therein could neither stand nor lie.

In another dungeon, sea valves could be opened to allow the slowly rising tide to fill the chamber. Slow death seemed to be the theme on which Santiago had been constructed. American prisoners sent there for trial usually waited from five to six months for their cases to appear before a "jury" of Japs.

Trials had but two verdicts, death or acquittal. My information of the prison came first-hand from a fellow who had spent five months there awaiting trial for his life. He had been captured by the Japs in Manila early in 1943, wearing civilian clothing and carrying the credentials of a Spanish doctor.

The Japs suspected him of being an American, and investigation revealed that he was a navy radioman. During the Corregidor campaign, his command had sent him into Manila to carry out guerilla activities on the piers of the city. Tons of foodstuffs and drugs were lying on the wharves, and this man's mission was to destroy as much of it as possible.

When Corregidor fell, he had no place to go, and had lived with friendly Filipinos in the city. When he was apprehended, his fate looked discouraging. He was cast into a dungeon at Santiago with thirteen other men and women awaiting trial for espionage.

They sat with arms and legs crossed in a circle in the center of the room under a ten-watt light globe for fifteen hours each day. They were forbidden to talk or whisper, and were fed one cup of rice and soup daily.

When this radioman's trial came up, he was extremely fortunate in the Japs' selection of his interpreter and defense counsel, for it proved to be a young Jap with whom the prisoner had attended the University of California in 1935. The defense counsel coached the accused man in detail prior to the trial, and he was promptly acquitted and sent to Bilibid to live the life of a common prisoner of war.

What the fate was of the unfortunate man who failed in his attempt to escape from Bilibid, I do not know. The fellow who succeeded, however, lived in the city of Manila until the return of American forces to the Philippines.

Not long ago while reading the Marine publication, *Leatherneck*, I was delighted to see his picture and read an account of his experiences.

On March 20, 1944, I was sent to Cabanatuan once more. My eyes were in fairly good condition again, and my general health had been improved by a year of rest. We traveled in typical prisoner style, via boxcar.

The headlight on the coconut-hull-burning locomotive was not functioning; to me, our night trip into the provinces seemed rather hazardous. Each time the train thundered over a bridge I said to myself, "Well, there's another bridge that the guerrillas haven't blown up!"

9 - RETURN TO CABANATUAN

CONDITIONS IN THE CENTRAL CAMP had improved greatly since I had left a year and a half before. Sanitary latrines had been constructed, and I was pleased to learn that the death rate had diminished to one man per month. Many of my old friends were still there, and we shared hours of laughs recalling old times. The Japanese had commandeered about ten square miles of land surrounding the camp which they had converted into a farm, using fifteen hundred American prisoners as laborers. Everything was done by hand with pick and shovel. The original virgin land was densely covered with brush and tropical quack grass eight feet tall.

The land was cleared with bolos by men working on their hands and knees in the cutting grass. Their only diversion was the occasional discovery of a cobra nest. The eggs, slipped into one's pocket, made a tasty supplement to his evening meal, but the prize catch was a mature cobra. If the Japs did not see the reptile first, it was quickly killed and skinned like a glove, the hide leaving the carcass and taking the intestinal organs with it.

The Japs, although realizing that their bite was deadly, displayed little fear in handling the snakes. After catching one, they removed its fangs with a pocket knife, and then placed it on the ground, allowing it to strike at them. After an hour of this tormenting, the snake was killed and placed in an empty mess kit for the Jap's evening meal.

We worked with bare feet daily on the farm. Much work was entailed, as each plant required fertilization and irrigation; all, of course, done with hand labor. After several weeks of working in the scorching sun, we made an agreement with the Japs whereby we went to work very early in the morning, had the afternoon off, and worked late into the evening.

Our new hours were 5.30 A.M. to twelve o'clock, and 3 P.M. to 7 P.M. The three-hour noon period gave us relief from the heat of the day.

On the farm we raised sweet potatoes, onions, eggplant, okra, and a Filipino version of spinach. The only crop harvested from which we were given any proceeds was the spinach. The remaining foodstuffs were sold by the Japs in the city of Manila at tremendous prices. With our longer periods of rest in the barracks we were enabled to pursue many pastimes, some of them illicit, such as sharpening the spring from the sole of an army shoe into razor sharpness for shaving, playing cards, and the like. Ofttimes while idling away the hours, men were caught off-guard smoking while lying down, or committing some other minor infraction of rules, by a roving Japanese sentry.

To avert this catastrophe, we established the following warning system: when a Jap entered our quarters, the first man seeing him called loudly, "Motors in the West!"

This byword announced the presence of a Jap; knives, matches, cards and money invariably disappeared in record time. This system of warning worked well until one day a guard entered the building unnoticed, stood in the doorway for a moment, then in broken English announced, "Motors in the West!"

Obviously, the sentry, having heard the phrase repeatedly upon his entrance into a building, considered it some sort of greeting. Nevertheless, we changed our warning to "Air Raid," and later, "Hobnails," and "Earthquake."

By now we had knowledge of the Japanese language; often while working, we would find ourselves under the custody of a friendly guard anxious to learn a little English. Most of them were curious and wanted to know all about life in America. One such talkative sentry opened his shirt one day and showed me a cross hanging from a small chain around his neck. My first idea was that he had taken it from some prisoner, but in broken English he told me that his parents had been killed in the Japanese earthquake in 1923, and that he had been raised in a Catholic orphanage.

With his knowledge of English and my meager understanding of Japanese, I learned many interesting things. He was a Christian, and was opposed to the brutal practices of his army, but could do nothing about them. In the months to come, I met several such soldiers who professed Christianity, but had their hands tied by being, as they expressed it, "in the wrong army."

Red Cross supplies arrived once from the States while I was interned in Cabanatuan. The Jap officials in charge of the camp took what they wanted before turning the goods over to us, but the soldiers who supervised our labor got nothing.

Of course, they knew we had small quantities of medicine, and as most of them suffered from advanced cases of gonorrhea, they were very anxious to procure sulfathiazole tablets. A few unscrupulous prisoners sold some of the precious pills to the Japs, thus establishing a market for the drug at exorbitant prices. Knowledge of the curative powers of sulfathiazole spread swiftly among their ranks, and soon the price had risen to twenty dollars a pill. Nearly every Jap guard began asking for the medicine; but, of course, we needed our meager supply for our own men.

Fellows unable to work went into the manufacturing business; making pills from cornstarch. These were baked and then engraved with a groove on one side and a "W" on the other. Thousands of these worthless tablets were sold to the Japs at tremendous prices.

Among the Red Cross supplies received was a small shipment of personal packages for prisoners from their families in America. The fortunate fellows who received such packages were called to Jap headquarters and ordered to open them before a censor. Any contraband was then confiscated, and the man returned to his quarters with his treasured possessions.

A friend of mine received such a package and was dismayed to find a carton of tooth powder had burst, covering the entire contents of the box with powder.

He wiped off the articles as best he could, showed them to the Jap and then returned to display them to his friends.

When emptying the contents of the box, he turned it upside down and discovered three copies of Reader's Digest in the bottom.

I believe that every man in camp read those precious bits of literature and from them learned of many Allied advances in various theaters of operation, of the discovery of penicillin, the development of radar, and many other invaluable pieces of information.

They served as a splendid lift to the morale of many men who thought they had been let down by their country.

During my last stay at Cabanatuan, a buddy and I procured a small plot of land in the rear of our quarters which we spaded and cultivated into a garden.

From the camp's farm we "obtained" seed and small plants, and in our leisure hours we fertilized and planted them with loving care.

Each night we watered it with several buckets of bathwater and inspected each plant, ascertaining its growth that day. Several other fellows in camp had small gardens, too, and fertilized them in the Jap method by using human offal from the latrines. My partner and I, however, used a method more American.

On our trips to and from the farm, we picked up dried cakes of carabao manure and carried them back to camp under our clothing. We learned about farming the hard way but finally had a beautiful crop of corn, onions, garlic, and sweet potatoes ready for an early harvest.

On June 15, 1944, just when our crops were nearing maturity, the Japs called for one thousand men to go to Japan. My name was drawn, and my gardening partner volunteered to go also so we could be together.

Our greatest regret was in leaving our garden behind. From our long hours of work, we realized about a dozen small onions; the remainder of the vegetables would mature within the month. We left Cabanatuan for Manila via train on the morning of June 20, and couldn't help but wonder what fate held in store for us.

At Manila, the man who volunteered to go on the Japan-bound trip with me was stricken with a kidney malfunction and his name was scratched from the sailing list. He recovered and sailed on the next prison ship, which was sunk by Allied submarines.

Such ships were common freighters flying the Japanese flag and were entirely unmarked concerning their human cargo. I feel certain that Allied submarine commanders would have spared prisoner-carrying vessels but had no way of ascertaining such freightage. Thousands of men who had survived the Death March and appalling years of prison life died in the Japs' attempt to evacuate them to their homeland prior to the American re-occupation of the Islands.

We spent two weeks in Manila at Bilibid Prison awaiting transport to Japan. A buddy and I recalled many of the good times we had had together upon being reunited in Bilibid. This fellow had lost the sight of one eye and was steadily going blind in the other, but the loss of his sight did not dull his optimism or sense of humor.

We both agreed that he, staying in the Philippines, would be liberated at least six months sooner than I in Japan. In view of this foresight, we exchanged mess kits with the agreement that, when he returned to the States, if I were not yet liberated, he would contact my parents and send them my mess kit engraved with my name and organization.

The pact was fulfilled for upon his liberation in the Philippines my parents received the kit and a letter from this loyal friend, who was being schooled in the reading of braille at a New York hospital for the blind. On July 2, 1944, we were informed that our ship was ready, and we were marched to the pier.

As we marched down Manila's Rizal Avenue, traffic halted, and the Filipinos lined the streets to watch us pass. From the interior of a cabaret, a jukebox blared loudly, "There's a Great Day Coming!"

10 - En Route to Dai Nippon

UPON ARRIVAL AT THE PIER, we found our ship to be a rusty freighter weighing about ten thousand tons. As we boarded her, we passed a plaque on the bridge labeling her the S.S. Canadian Inventor, built and launched in Vancouver, British Columbia, in 1920. She had been captured by the Japs in Singapore and was still manned by her original pro-British Chinese crew. These crewmen had been terrorized to such an extent that they didn't dare glance at our group of prisoners.

Given the opportunity, however, I feel certain that they would have been friendly toward us, but they, as the Filipinos, fraternized with American prisoners only under the threat of capital punishment. Far below the waterline between storage holds, the thousands of us were cramped into quarters too small to allow all of us to sit or lie down at the same time.

When the first seven hundred men filled the space, the remaining three hundred were forced into the compartment at the point of fixed bayonets. That night we weighed anchor and cleared Manila Bay en route to the Land of the Rising Sun. After being underway for about six hours, however, we felt the ship make an abrupt turn; then we sailed full speed toward Manila Bay once more. Perhaps we had been sighted by Allied submarines; at any rate, for the following two weeks, our foul craft rocked at anchor in the bay under the merciless tropical sun.

We were fed twice daily; meals consisted of a cup of rice and a cup of tea. Even when we were at sea this menu did not vary except for the missing of meals completely during inclement weather. At the end of two weeks we got underway once more, the holds of the ship empty of cargo. After twenty-five days of rough seas, zigzagging, and tremendous rocking due to lack of ballast, we docked at a port called Takao, Formosa.

During the entire trip, I did not have a bowel movement and had emptied my bladder but few times.

Perhaps it was just as well, however, as sanitary facilities were primitive, to say the least; two five-gallon cans served one thousand men and were emptied twice daily, weather permitting, by being pulled to the deck with ropes. When being hauled up, the swaying cans struck the sides of the ship and were usually over half empty upon reaching the deck. Needless to say, they made quite a mess of the unfortunate men below. When I consulted a doctor regarding my intestinal inactivity, he comforted me with the information that he was beginning the nineteenth day of the same predicament.

Every bit of food which we consumed was utilized almost immediately by our bodies. The suffocating heat of the ship caused us to sweat constantly, and our bodies were fast becoming dehydrated. By the time we reached Formosa, nearly a third of the men were ill, requiring space to lie down; consequently, those of us who were well were forced to stand constantly, resting occasionally by kneeling for a few minutes.

The boilers of the ship were in such a dilapidated condition that the Japs refused to enter the engine room. One Japanese engineer supervised the firing of the furnaces done by American prisoners. These stokers had been recruited from our group by promises of extra rice. Seven times during the first lap of our voyage the boilers had burst, causing a delay in mid-ocean until makeshift repairs enabled steam pressure to be built up once more. At Formosa we lay rotting in the bay for another two weeks while native coolies loaded the ship with a cargo of salt.

During our layover the smell ascending from our hold was of such a malodorous nature that it moved even the Japs, who made arrangements for us to bathe and hose out our quarters. A rope ladder was suspended from the deck of the ship to a pier where a fire hose gushed gallons of cold, fresh water. While washing, I rinsed my clothing contrary to orders by using them piece by piece as wash clothes. I even washed my shoes because they were moldy and infested with lice and bedbugs. When ascending the Jacob's ladder, my wet clothing and shoes made too cumbersome a burden, so I shouted to a friend on deck, to whom I tossed the bundle. Of course, he failed to catch it and it fell into the ocean between the ship and the pier.

Visions flashed through my mind of making the rest of the voyage and of debarking in Japan stark naked, so I shouted to a sentry, drawing his attention to my fast-sinking clothing and, without waiting for his consent, I dove into the water after the precious bundle.

I succeeded in recovering the clothing and threw them onto the dock. Then I wished someone were there to throw me out, too, as the five-foot cement wall from the water to the top of the pier offered no better footing than the barnacle-encrusted side of the ship.

Two friends, observing my plight, managed to pull me out; but in the effort I scratched myself severely on the cement walls of the dock. After I had reached the deck once more, someone drew my attention to the fact that the ship had drifted flush against the pier, and how fortunate I was in getting out when I did. For the first time the hold of the ship looked good to me. Not only had the bath been a refreshing treat to us but was obviously a source of great entertainment to the giggling and pointing populace of the port town who had turned out en masse to witness the skinny, naked American prisoners bathe. We were more than glad to get underway again and, after numerous breakdowns and several scares from Allied submarines, we docked on the southern tip of Japan at a port called Moji.

We had lost but one man on the entire trip, but all of us were in such a weakened condition that we, with eyes smarting in the unaccustomed daylight, staggered down the gangplank like a bunch of drunkards. By the time we disembarked, the ship was alive with bedbugs and body lice. Because of the constant heat and sweating, our skins were broken out with heat-rash. Next to having all the fresh water we wanted to drink, our idea of Heaven was a place where we could bathe.

Several Japanese port officials boarded the ship at the pier in Moji and inspected us. They stood on the deck looking down into the hold and talking with one another. As we mounted the deck in preparation to disembarking, a Jap officer asked one of our men what sort of trip he had had from the Philippines.

The man (a colonel) didn't pull any punches in his description and ended his vehement delineation of the voyage by saying it was a miracle that any of us was still alive.

The Jap merely smiled and replied, "We Japanese know to the exact degree the extent of human endurance. Before you are liberated, you will learn that. You will see that we know how to beat a man to within an inch of his life and when one more blow will kill him. We also know how many grains of rice are required for a prisoner to live and work for one day."

In the year that followed, I thought more than once of this officer's statement and realized how right he had been. As we marched down the gangplank, a Jap soldier, operating a fly spray can, vaporized us with a chemical; the method of disinfecting in Dai Nippon Keikoku[14].

---

[14] Imperial Japanese Commonwealth.

11 - THE LAND OF THE RISING SUN

AFTER LEAVING THE SHIP we were paraded down the main street of Moji; an execrable-looking procession, dirty, thin, staggering, and every man with a two-months' growth of beard. Strangely enough, the civilians on the streets did not make fun of us, but merely watched as we passed, their faces set stoically in typical Oriental fashion. We were herded into the site of a former stable, given plenty of water and a cup of rice and then informed that the following morning we would be split into groups of one hundred and fifty men and sent to various remote camps.

That night I stretched out full length on the sawdust-covered ground and literally drank in the fresh air. It was a grand feeling, lying there watching the stars and clouds and not having to fight for every breath. After that sixty-two-day luxury cruise from Manila to Japan, suffering every kind of deprivation, we were glad to be alive to enjoy such comforts as fresh air and cool water.

We were aroused before daybreak the following morning, divided into one hundred- and fifty-man groups, and assigned to our respective camps. My group, we were informed by an interpreter assigned to our company, was destined for a rural mining community in Central Honshu; our train would leave in an hour.

For the first time since having been taken prisoner I enjoyed the luxury of day-coach travel. Our party sat two men to each seat in two coaches. We were pleased to note that our mode of travel was even better than that provided civilian passengers, as passing trains were packed with travelers standing in the aisles and in the doorways. Our interpreter, not knowing that we possessed a fair knowledge of the Japanese language, carried on a conversation with the train's conductor. He instructed him that, when we neared certain military objectives, munition plants, and naval bases, he was to draw the blinds to obstruct our vision of them. He stopped short in his conversation when observing all of us listening to him attentively.

Later in the day, he attempted to converse with several of us in Japanese; but to him we knew only one word, "Wakarumosen," meaning, "I do not understand."

Twice daily during the thirty-six-hour ride, the train stopped at pre-designated points and took on small wooden boxes of rice and cooked vegetables. Each man was given a box as his ration. Women on the railway platform filled our canteen cups with hot tea as we extended them from the train windows. After a day and a half of the train's laboring through mountain passes and tunnels, we disembarked at a point high in the mountains where we were to transfer to a narrow-gauge railway.

While waiting for our train to be made up, we witnessed a "Banzai," or going-away ceremony for a young, prospective soldier whose relatives and friends had gathered at the railroad station to bid him farewell. The boy blushed deeply when saying "sayonara" (since it must be so, or goodbye) to his parents while his friends cheered loudly. The train from which we were unloaded carried the young soldier away to war.

"The irony of fate," I thought to myself, "us arriving humble, defeated, a vanquished group of soldiers to work as slave laborers for this pagan race, and the young soldier, eager, patriotic, yearning for adventure, departing from the community in which he had been raised."

I still wonder what fate held in store for that fellow. In the two-hour course of our ride through the mountains on the narrow-gauge railway, we made several stops for switching. At one such stopping place, I noticed a prosperous-appearing home on the hillside where an elderly woman was standing in the doorway. She, calling to our guards, inquired if we were soldiers. Their reply was, *"Ni, horyo."* (No, prisoners.)

The fact that we were prisoners, and consequently an enemy, did not daunt this woman, however, as she left her house and came down to wave and smile at us, wishing us a happy trip. That mother's smile did more to boost our morale than any other incident in months. As the train left again, I glanced back to see her still waving and noticed that the Japanese flag flying from the house had the peak of the staff draped in black. The flag designated a son in service; the black-draped peak signified that he had been killed.

It was then that I realized that mothers are alike the world over. Had a trainload of Japanese prisoners passed my home in America, I felt certain that my mother would have reacted in much the same manner. The flatcars on which we rode were nothing but dwarfed freight cars and, while passing through tunnels, we were drenched with water dripping from overhead. However, we were a dirty lot anyway, and a little water, more or less, did not make much difference.

As we neared the village of Funatsu, the guards pointed out a stockade high on the mountainous slope across the river and informed us that it was to be our new home. Approaching the place, we were curious to know who was waving to us from the barred windows of the buildings. We asked the guards, but they didn't know. Their job was to deliver us to the authorities in charge of the camp, which they did in short order after we left the train.

As our party approached the walled-in stockade, the doors swung open and we were counted like sheep as we entered. As instructed, we formed columns of fours and listened to a speech in Japanese by the camp commander which was translated for us in perfect English by a little Jap wearing civilian clothing. His idiom ran along the following line:

"Today is the fourth day, ninth month of the year 2,604, or nineteenth year of Showa."[15] The interpreter began with: "That was the 'old man' talking to you, fellas, and what he says is law. He's a tough old bird and has seen more action than any of you. A quick way for any of you to lose your heads is to cross the old boy up, etc."

We learned that the young interpreter was born and raised in Honolulu and had graduated from the University of Hawaii.

---

[15] Time years in Japan are computed beginning with the coronation of the first emperor, Jinmu, in 660 BC. The year of Showa begins with the year of the reign of the present emperor. "Showa" means "Era of enlightened harmony."

Upon the outbreak of war, he was studying for his Ph.D. at the University of Tokyo. Friendly as this man was, however, he never once confided in us his political views nor did he express his opinions regarding the outcome of the war. Prior to entering the building, which was to be our home, we were ordered into the bathhouse for a much-needed scrubbing.

We found exceedingly cold water in a two-hundred-gallon wooden tank in the center of the room which was filled by buckets from a nearby mountain spring. We scrubbed with sand in lieu of soap and emerged from the bathhouse clean; all but for our two-months growth of whiskers.

Upon entering the barracks, we found it partitioned off; one half for our group and the other for a group of two hundred British prisoners captured at Singapore and Thailand. We were in such a weakened condition that work was out of the question for the time being. We were informed that for the following two weeks we could rest and clean up our badly soiled clothing. During those two weeks we learned the Japanese version of military drill and calisthenics.

Upon arising at 5 A.M., we exercised under the supervision of a Jap soldier. This same instructor taught us the fundamentals of drill for four hours daily. Once having learned the commands and movements, including the goose-step, we used them daily for roll-call formations and when going to and from work in the factory.

For the following year, I drilled and commanded a group of thirty-seven men in Japanese. During our two-week period of rest and recuperation, we became acquainted with our fellow Allied prisoners, the British. Their group was composed of two hundred English and Scots, two Australians, and one Canadian, who told us of the fall of Singapore and of their voyage to Japan three months prior to our arrival. In their convoy of three prison ships, two had been sunk by Allied submarines. Needless to say, these fellows felt thankful and lucky to be alive. The Japs forbade contact between the Americans and British, but, naturally, we mingled and discussed war news almost at will.

From our billet on the mountainside, we had an uninterrupted view of the entire mining community.

The district was surrounded by towering mountains located on the sides of a river which flowed through the valley. These mountains were of such height that the sun shone only from 10 A.M. until 2 P.M. daily. We didn't mind the absence of the sun in the early fall, but as the days grew colder, we began to miss it more and more. The community was composed of laborers' hovels and lead and zinc mines on the side of one of the mountains. The ore extracted therefrom was sent down the slope by cable cars to the factories in the valley.

One of these factories was called "Shoko Ryoson" (acid factory), where sulphuric acid was extracted from the ore through a baking process; then it was transported by narrow-gauge railway cars to a neighboring plant called "Ion Denki" (electric smelting). In its final processing at Ion Denki, the ore was chemically treated and transformed into plates of zinc, which in turn were smelted down into eight-kilo ingots. Our group was divided into three work parties, each with a foreman in charge. I was fortunate in being elected the supervisor of my group.

On our first day at the factory, we were watched with considerable interest by the Jap civilian employees, many of whom had never before seen an American. Most of these employees were women and children and men too old for military service. At first, we were guarded too closely for any contact; but as the days passed, we won the confidence of our guards and were often left for the entire day to work unguarded except for factory overseers who made occasional rounds inspecting our work.

When these people first attempted to talk to us, we were rather hesitant in answering, for the Japanese we knew had been taught us by Jap soldiers in the Philippines, and the fact that soldiers often speak in shady vernaculars pressed heavily on our minds. Just what kind of language had we been taught by those soldiers?

Was it fit for conversation with women and children? Stepping off to a very cautious beginning, we soon learned that we spoke the same language; every word we knew was acceptable in their society. There is no cursing or risqué slang in the Japanese tongue. The strongest expression of verbal rebuke is calling one "bakanna" (stupid), "inu" (dog), "buta" (pig), etc.

Japanese women have many redeeming qualities. Although they are dominated by the superior males, when given the opportunity they express many forms of sympathy and kindness.

In typical Oriental fashion they carry their children strapped to their backs. I have often wondered what prevented their little necks from breaking as their heads bobbed to and fro in rhythm with the mother's gait. High in rural mountainous Japan, I observed the most flawless, feminine complexions imaginable, and all without the aid of cosmetics. The women do not smoke or drink, work out-of-doors most of the time, and get plenty of rest. These factors, together with the complete absence of dissipation, contribute greatly to their natural beauty. I have often thought how the women of America could learn a lesson in pulchritude from the unsophisticated daughters of Nippon.

After I had worked in the factory for a week, a car of ore ran over my right foot. Fortunately, no bones were broken. The flesh was cut, and ligaments torn; but by staying off it for a month, it healed. During that time of convalescence, I made a pair of woolen mittens from a portion of an old blanket, since each day was colder than the one preceding and I knew that the time would soon arrive when I would need them.

Our barracks were made of plywood and were very poorly constructed. The Japs made no attempt to install heating equipment, and it looked like a cold winter ahead.

In November, an earthquake shook the entire valley. When it began, I found myself standing under a seventy-five-foot brick smokestack which swayed like a buggy whip. My first impulse was to run clear of the pendulum-like stack, but I reached the conclusion that I would endanger my life more that way than by standing directly at its base and determining in which direction it would fall. After what seemed an eternity, the quake stopped and the smoke-stack was still standing. Why, I'll never know.

Late in that same month, most of the men had pooled their thin blankets with two other fellows and slept three together, changing positions during the night in an effort to keep warm. Long, narrow shelves running in two tiers the length of the building served as beds. There is little doubt that working saved the lives of most of the men in the camp that winter because at the factory we had the opportunity to get warm once in a while.

Our usual task was transporting a given number of tons of ore from an outdoor bin to a furnace and then unloading it into a conveyor-pit which carried it to the upper floors of the ramshackle plant. When the task was completed, the balance of the nine-hour shift was devoted to resting beside a red-hot coke stove. We alternated day and night shift, changing every ten days. During the winter's severest weeks, the night shift was the more popular with the men for, if they completed their work by midnight, they were permitted to sleep until 4 A.M., the time to return to camp.

After a breakfast consisting of a cup of watery, cooked rice, the night workers slept through the day, and thus were spared much of winter's bite. Shortly after the first snowfall, American Red Cross food packages arrived in the valley for the Allied prisoners of war.

One night after work, we carried these boxes from the railroad station to the camp. Upon their arrival in camp they were stored in a warehouse and we wondered when our hosts would see fit to present them to us. It was a gnawing sensation, being hungry and knowing that only a few feet away was good American food sent to us by our own people.

Finally, on Christmas Day, 1944, each man was given a twelve-pound box containing several cans of meat, a half-pound of cubed sugar, six ounces of chocolate, dried fruit, and a half dozen packages of cigarettes. It was indeed a joyous Christmas. The Japs gave us the day off at the factory, and everyone stuffed himself with the type of food on which he had been raised. Our barracks were so cold that we spent the day under blankets, but morale was high, and we were happy. My bed partner and I smoked two packages of Camels that day, being very careful, however, to place the butts in a can, knowing that the following week we'd be breaking them up and re-rolling them.

During the following six months we were issued the remaining Red Cross supplies in scant quantities, often two or three men sharing a can of corned beef. Every two weeks a completely new company of Japanese guards assumed sentry duty in our camp. The only exception was in the case of the officer in command and members of his staff. This permutation, as nearly as I could ascertain, was to prevent our becoming too familiar with any of them.

These guards were combat veterans with minor disabilities such as battle fatigue, the loss of several fingers, or some other incapacity rendering them useless for further combat duty. Such a change of guards was affected on Christmas Day.

The corporal of the new guard company, a stocky fellow wearing heavily rimmed glasses, entered our barracks that cold morning on a routine tour of inspection. After looking around, observing men eating chocolate and smoking American cigarettes, he announced in fairly good English that he had eaten that type of food during his school days at the Imperial University.

Pursuant to our usual custom of pumping any friendly Jap for war news, we did not let this fellow leave the building without interrogation. He seemed willing to talk and appeared to be better informed regarding Allied movements than any Jap we had met thus far. I stationed a man at the door of the barracks to watch for the sergeant of the guard or Jap commander, drew the sentry's attention to the fact that we had a look-out posted, and invited him to sit down and smoke a Camel with me. With the stump of an illicit pencil, I drew a rough map of the Orient inside the cover of my New Testament, then handed him the pencil and book, asking him to draw a line showing the Allied advance in the Pacific. He hesitated and then proceeded to do as I asked.

His drawing looked rather discouraging at first, but further questioning revealed that America had conducted long-distance aerial attacks on the Japanese home islands and had land-based planes within range of the Archipelago.

In compliance with my request, he marked the locations of the "Shima" (islands) where these planes were based. From his crude sketching, I construed them to be the Marshall and Mariana groups. When the guard finished his cigarette, he left, cautioning me not to repeat any of the information he had narrated and reminding me that both he and I would be decapitated if the authorities learned the nature of our conversation. Had the Red Cross supplies failed to raise my morale that day, that bit of war news certainly would have helped. I slept that night, dreaming of home and feeling certain that on the following Christmas I would be home with my family.

After Christmas a severe cold spell set in, bringing sickness to many of the men whose resistance had been lowered by previous months of hardships. By spring, we had lost thirteen of our group of one hundred and fifty men. Their bodies were cremated at the community pyre in the village, and their ashes placed in vials on shelves in the Japanese camp office.

Late in January, the Japanese officer in command of the camp called five of us into his office, offered us cigarettes and tea, and then gathered us around his small charcoal fire.

Through the interpreter, he informed us that his country needed him on a fighting front and that he was leaving the camp in charge of a master sergeant, whom he introduced to us at that time. He thanked us for our cooperation while under his jurisdiction and wished us good health and early freedom. With that he departed.

Nothing changed much under the new administration, but treatment from the guards for minor infractions of rules seemed much more humane. One evening, after two weeks of his reign, our new camp commander summoned five of us to his office and informed us that the valley was snow-blocked from the outside world as the result of the most severe winter in twenty years.

He told us that there was a meager food supply in the valley which must be carefully rationed if we prisoners and the civilian populace were to survive until spring when the railroad would run again.

"I realize," he said, "that your diet is not ample for the nature of your work or the condition of your health, but there is nothing I can do about it." He went on to say, "Through the fortunes of war, you have become my prisoners. But for the grace of your God or mine, I might have been your prisoner; and had such an event transpired, I would expect the same humane treatment which I am endeavoring to bestow on you."

"My eyes," he continued, "are brown and slanted, yours are blue and straight; but we see the same things. We have the same desires, appetites, and emotions. Cooperate with me and I will do everything within my limited power to treat you as human beings."

That conference left me a little dazed. For the first time in my life as a prisoner, I realized that there were a few Japs whose minds ran in the same channel as those of Occidentals. During the weeks to follow, the new commander demanded and received strict obedience to every order and in turn did his best to alleviate our suffering. When one of my men at the factory was maltreated by a civilian employee of the concern, I reported the incident to the commander, who early the following morning mounted his bicycle and headed for the factory.

After a thorough investigation of the incident, he reprimanded the offender with a whipping by using the flat side of his flexible saber. Thereafter such conduct on the part of civilian Japs was rare. Unfortunately, this western-minded non-commissioned officer was called to a fighting front, and the camp was turned over to a "Junshikwan" (warrant officer).

This new commander, we learned from his campaign ribbons, had fought in China, Singapore, Bataan, and New Guinea, and had been wounded. He walked with a slight limp and appeared to have the use of only one eye. On occasion he shouted orders to us but refused to talk with any prisoner, even the American officer in charge of our camp.

During the brutal winter, most of our shoes were completely worn out. By placing cardboard and even wooden shingles in the bottoms, we managed to keep from being completely barefooted. Much of the time, however, we worked in water at the factory; consequently, our shoes were either wet or frozen all during the winter. From Christmas until late in June, my feet were dead-numb as the result of frostbite and beriberi; my toenails were black.

Often at night, when the work quota had been filled and we sat around the stove warming ourselves, I attempted to dry my shoes and to restore feeling in my feet. It proved useless, however; when my feet came in too close contact with the stove, I could smell them scorching but experienced no sensation. I wondered if, when they completely thawed out, I would have any feet left. As the result of sleeping in our clothes and general unsanitary conditions, we were plagued with lice.

Every ten days, just before changing from night to day shift, I heated a bucket of water on the stove in our shack at the factory and enjoyed the luxury of a hot bath. When finished with the water, I used it to boil out the lice in my clothing. More than once on a cold winter night, while huddling by the stove waiting for my clothes to dry and clad only in a G-string, one of the Jap bosses would enter the room and demand that I make a tour of inspection over the plant where the men were working. When I returned, my wet clothing was frozen stiff.

At times during the hard winter, many of the men let conditions get them down. While making a tour of the plant to check on the men at their various jobs, I often found some poor fellow crying in despair. When such a situation arose, I took the man from his task and brought him back to our crude rest-shack. After giving him a cup of hot water and a cigarette (if I happened to have one) and letting him thoroughly warm himself by the stove, I talked to the man, telling him all (and often more) of the latest war news I had heard.

I would tell him that we were certain to be free before the following Christmas and tried to get him to agree with me on that point. Then I would lapse into my favorite morale-building argument about American insurance companies computing the average longevity rate at fifty-five years.

Asking the man his age (which was usually around twenty-four) I pointed out to him that, by being liberated within the next year, he would have at least thirty years of the American way of living ahead of him, never having to suffer from cold or hunger, and that everything he had ever wanted to live for would be his.

Usually about an hour of this sort of pep-talk did the trick, and the man returned to his job with renewed spirit.

Then I would begin to wonder myself just when we would get out of this mess. However, in my position it would never do to appear down-hearted. Often at night, with the blankets covering my head, and wondering if my numb feet were under them or out in the cold, I wished that I had someone around to cheer me up a bit, too.

My armband gave me the authority to go many places that were "off limits" to the other prisoners in the factory. Especially at night after our work had been completed, I wandered through various parts of the plant, such as the machine shop, chemical laboratory, and Japanese rest-shack. I became well acquainted with many *kojo*,[16] most of whom were quite curious about Americans.

Prior to the war, they had all attended American movies and were acquainted with the names of most of the Hollywood stars. American movies shown in Japan were talkies, and to the right of the screen was a caption translating the conversation into Japanese. Unfortunately, as most moviegoers will agree, American films portray a comparatively gay mode of life instead of actual existing conditions.

Rarely does the hero or heroine of a movie work for a living but usually leads a merry life of lounging around night clubs, cocktail lounges, operas, and private yachts. More than one Jap has asked me if it is true that Americans rise around noon each day, have a couple of drinks before lunch, and then depart to the neighborhood dance hall for the remainder of the day and evening.

This sounds rather foolish, but taking into consideration their only view of American life, the movies, together with the Jap propaganda regarding the frivolity and laziness of our

---

[16] Factory girls.

race, one can comprehend the attitude of these simple peasants.

All of my time in wandering around the plant, however, was not devoted to correcting warped impressions of Americanism. Many of the plant employees were university students who were compelled to fulfill a period of servitude in one of Nippon's industrial efforts between certain years of their educational careers.

Many of these young students were friendly and well-informed regarding war activities. One fellow in particular, the son of a wealthy wine merchant in one of Japan's principal cities, brought his lunch wrapped in the daily newspaper.

The paper often contained war maps with figures of American planes based on certain islands of which I promptly inquired the names and made mental pictures of their locations.

Toward spring the news became better and better. These printed maps showed islands close to Japan studded with four-motored planes. The Jap told me of the horrible, new, aerial weapon which America was employing against them, called "B-niju ku" (B-29). My informant now read me the paper nightly. I often wondered what method of manslaughter the Japs would have chosen; had we been discovered poring over the daily paper.

From him I learned the exact date of D-Day, V-E Day, knew of Roosevelt's death the day it transpired, of MacArthur's return to the Philippines, and could clearly see that Japan was gradually being enveloped. I had been told by my informant that the Japanese Army had been instructed to kill every Allied prisoner immediately in the event of an invasion of Japan. Needless to say, I did not reiterate this bit of information to a living soul, and felt very uneasy when in July we heard the coast of the homeland being shelled constantly, hour after hour, for I had been taught that shell-fire against beach installations could mean but one thing: softening them up for invasion.

Fortunately, the Allied air forces either did not know of the existence of the acid factory where we worked or considered it too insignificant to attack.

At any rate, we were not bombed during the war. We had an air raid siren in the valley which sounded one long blast whenever a raid took place in the Empire. In the event of a raid within a three-hundred-mile radius, five short blasts were sounded and everyone in the valley sought the protection of a shelter.

By spring, the siren was either announcing a raid or sounding the all-clear signal nearly every hour of the day and night. Several times during night raids, flights of American planes passed over the valley, filling it with vibrations.

I was anxious to see the ship that the Japs had described as such a formidable weapon and that was heavy enough to vibrate the earth when it passed overhead. With the coming of spring, a Japanese general made an inspection tour of our camp. We were notified to prepare for the inspection two weeks in advance and, on the day prior to his arrival, we were relieved from work at the factory to ready our quarters.

We scrubbed the floors, walls, and ceilings, raked the yard, repaired broken shutters, and dug air raid shelters.

On the morning of his arrival, we all shaved with our mess kit knives—a trick learned and perfected in the Philippines—and watched four quarters of beef being carried into the kitchen.

That afternoon the cauldrons were filled with steaming rice; one corner of the kitchen was stacked with sacked vegetables, and from the rafters hung the four quarters of beef. When the general passed through the kitchen, he must have been impressed by the way we were being fed.

He had been gone from the camp for less than ten minutes when the kitchen was cleared of all show material, including the meat and vegetables. The rice that had been cooked, the Japs informed us, would suffice for two of the following days' meals.

In his personal inspection of the prisoners the general had an interpreter at his side, but did not utilize his services. He looked at each man, and frequently asked questions.

Of me he inquired my age. When I informed him that it was twenty-five, he asked why my hair was gray, to which I replied "malnutrition."

However, after having been through the kitchen and seeing how well we were being fed, he merely grunted and passed on. He created an impressive sight, neatly attired in full uniform, looking like anything but an Oriental, and speaking in perfect English. Before dismissing us from ranks, he inquired if any of us had attended West Point. No one had, but his query led me to infer that perhaps he had at one time.

With the exception of food, perhaps my greatest desire was for music. In the Philippines we were fortunate in having men in our group who were richly endowed with musical talent. Among our vocalists was a man who had sung with Tommy Dorsey's orchestra. We had one of Bunny Berigan's top pianists who played beautifully on a burned and rebuilt piano at Cabanatuan.

It was not until I arrived in Japan and was completely cut off from the world of music that I detected an inner longing for familiar strains. My propensity found an outlet through the medium of slumber in an absurd but satisfying manner. Often during the long, cold winter nights, I dreamed of sitting in a large concert hall with a symphony orchestra in the process of tuning-up. Then followed a two- or three-hour concert of symphonic music which kept me on the edge of my seat, clutching the program sheet. Invariably, at the end of the recital, I awoke exhausted.

However, I thoroughly enjoyed each session and eagerly anticipated the next. The climax of my dream-concerts was reached one night when a phantasmal conductor led his musicians in a two-hour rendition of Ravel's "Bolero."

12 - THE SETTING OF THE SUN

IN CHARGE OF PRISONER PERSONNEL at the factory was a retired Jap army officer, a man of shrewd intelligence and
worldly knowledge. He made no attempt to speak English. He
was the sort of man one rarely meets whose piercing eyes
make one uneasy in his presence. When he questioned me regarding the work my men had done or were performing, he
seemed to have an uncanny faculty of determining whether or
not I spoke the truth.

One night in early summer he summoned me to his office,
offered me a cigarette, and proceeded to question me regarding
the trend of current war news. He asked me how Germany
was faring in the war. I replied that I did not know. However,
he sensed that there was a leak of information somewhere in
the plant, and refused to believe that I was completely igno-
rant of important happenings.

Finally, I explained that I was only a prisoner of war, knew
nothing other than what had been told me by my superiors,
and entertained only thoughts pertaining to the nature of my
work. He did not believe a word of what I said and bluntly told
me so, but was unable to produce any tangible evidence that I
was being informed regarding the progress of the war.

With the arrival of summer, our camp commander made a
lend-lease arrangement for a garden plot about twelve miles
from camp. Knowing that I would become seriously involved in
an espionage charge if I remained at the factory and gathered
war news, I volunteered to take over the farm group.

It was fairly pleasant diversion walking and working in the
sun, all the while breathing clean, fresh air, and taking an occasional swim in a nearby river. We spent six hours daily
walking to and from work, and four actually working. The
Japs are born farmers, and have definite ideas regarding
planting, fertilizing, and rotating of crops. We fertilized the soil
with human waste from the village outhouses. This operation
was referred to by our group of Yanks as "the honey detail."

In our daily walk we observed a great deal of Japanese rural life. Every inch of ground was under cultivation; even the hillsides had been terraced in an effort to raise a few more vegetables. These people had devised a clever system of crop rotation beginning in the spring with rice which ripened in middle summer. Following the rice harvest, barley, which matures in middle fall, is planted. Just before the first frost, turnips and radishes are planted, and usually are harvested after the first snowfall of the season. The aforementioned radishes are indeed a novelty. Known in Japan as "daikon," they grow to tremendous proportions. One of these radishes, two feet in length and five inches in diameter at its base, is not uncommon.

Likewise, turnips the size of large grapefruit are conventional. Japan seems to provide fertile soil for many types of growth. On the mountainous slopes of Central Honshu, I was amazed to find oak, walnut, bamboo, northern pine, apricot, and plum trees. The latitude of this section of the Orient is 35 degrees, comparable to that of Oklahoma; yet many feet of snow and sub-freezing temperatures fail to daunt these hearty plants, many of which I considered semi-tropical.

In addition to raising foodstuffs, the Japs are skilled in the cultivation of dwarfed plants. Imagine, if you can, a backyard laid out to resemble a pine forest with the tallest mature tree measuring two feet in height, or an orchard of apple trees three feet in height bearing fruit. Occasionally while walking to and from work in our garden, we apprehended a snake crossing the trail. The life expectancy of such reptiles was short when a group of hungry prisoners was on hand, for when skinned and roasted over an open fire they provided a choice delicacy and the only source of protein we had.

Not only did we become adept in the hunting and cooking of snakes, but learned that many wild ferns and flowers were fit for human consumption and supplied our bodies with much-needed vitamins A and C. For each day we worked, fifteen sen were credited to our accounts in the camp commissary. Twice during our entire year in Japan, we were permitted to purchase goods through this company store.

Once in the fall, each man bought two apples for twenty-five sen; in the middle of the winter we were given the opportunity to purchase dried, powdered grass-hoppers. Each man bought several cupfuls and used them on his rice as a condiment. In taste this Oriental delicacy resembled a superior grade of sawdust with a fishy smell. To show their appreciation of our work, the factory officials occasionally provided us with a treat. One day in early February, they presented to us a box of dog entrails with the heart, kidney, and liver removed. We boiled the lungs, intestines, and stomach into a soup which received added body from a quantity of cooked rice found in the esophagus. In the spring when the local crop of cabbages was harvested, we were given the outer stripped leaves to boil into a soup. How I would have enjoyed pushing some Nip's face into that box of dog guts or cramming the spoiled cabbage, leaf by leaf, down his throat; but I was compelled to accept the gift, hiss my arigato, and leave the room.

Each day our walk to and from work took us through the village of Funatsu, and we were an untiring source of amusement to the natives who never failed to emerge from their homes and shops to watch us pass. Little children often ran after us shouting, "Horyo, Horyo," (prisoners), but the adults merely watched us with set facial expressions. There were no men of military age left in the village, all having been called to war. Practically every house was flying the Imperial flag, designating it as the home of a serviceman, and the black hoods on the peaks, denoting the death of a soldier, became more numerous as the months passed.

The Japanese countryside is dotted with shrines marked by the traditional arch with sagging crossbar as seen in nearly every pictorial view of the country. In these shrines are small statues of Shinto gods, headstones for departed ancestors, and receptacles containing the ashes of the family dead. Cremation is a firmly rooted institution in the Empire, introduced because of lack of burial space.

As previously mentioned, the bodies of our prisoner of war personnel were cremated and their ashes neatly bottled and labeled for return to America at the end of the war. In the

Philippines when Japanese soldiers died or were killed and cremation was impracticable, they were buried in a standing position in graves three feet in diameter and six feet in depth. This, too, seems to be a space-saving measure as small head-markers require much less area than a full-length grave.

With the arrival of spring and early summer, food became scarcer instead of plentiful as had been promised when the snow-bound railway was reopened. Our hosts did not hesitate to inform us that Allied submarines had accounted for thousands of tons of Jap shipping, and the little food they could now import came from Manchuria. Soybeans replaced rice in our diet; three times daily we were given a cup of beans devoid of salt or any condiment. The high altitude of our camp, the extremely hard water, and the natural toughness of soybeans made them difficult to cook. To make them digestible required eight hours of constant boiling; consequently, our small staff of cooks worked day and night preparing meals.

As the air raid alarm became more active, many Jap civilians left their urban homes and moved into rural communities. I noted a marked distinction between the cosmopolitan and rural Japs, the former being more sophisticated and better dressed than their agrarian brothers.

A few such migrants, braving the wrath of our guards as we passed through the village, called to us in English such things as, "Hi, boys," etc. The shortage of food supplies affected not only the prisoners, but also the factory officials who had been disgustingly healthy the previous autumn, and had now grown thin and haggard. Employees of the factory, en route to work, clutched pathetically small rice balls for their midday meal. The real tragedy of the situation, however, manifested itself in the effects of malnutrition on small children.

Their little bodies were thin and frail with contrasting pot-bellies, denoting the effects of beriberi and rickets. Mothers, preparing rice and vegetables for their families, washed each grain, leaf, and stem, making certain that only the dirt was washed down the stream where they were cleaned.

13 - The End

ON THE NIGHT OF AUGUST 12, 1945, the air raid alarm in the valley blew every three minutes with no let-up the following day. At midnight on the 13th of August, one long blast sounded which lasted over five minutes; something entirely new to the community, and we wondered what it could mean.

For the following three days no alarm sounded; but in passing through the village, we noticed groups of civilians gathered on corners and talking excitedly. Frequently, as we approached such groups, the words "Sinsu Wari" (war is ended) reached our ears. The very atmosphere of the community had changed, and we sensed something. On the morning of August 17, we fell out for work as usual, commenting on the fact that we hadn't heard an alarm for fifty-six hours. The guards who called for us at camp and brought us back at the end of the day arrived that morning as usual; but instead of escorting us to work, they were summoned into the Japanese office for a consultation which lasted an hour.

After we had impatiently stood in ranks for that long hour, the camp commander dismissed us, declaring that there would be no work that day because of a "Japanese holiday."

The factory man whom I mentioned a short while back, and who had questioned me at length regarding my knowledge of war news, was on hand that morning to take the party to the factory. As he was about to leave the compound he turned back and walked toward me. With a twinkle in his eye and an oh-so-wise look, he said to me, "Sayonara, kwaho mono."[17] To me those words meant, "Goodbye, Reynolds, the war is over and you're practically on your way home!"

I returned to the quarters filled with elation, then a horrible thought struck me. The Japs considered a person fortunate who died in the service of his country. The shelling of the coast had ceased, and perhaps the invasion which

---

[17] "Goodbye, lucky person."

would be our death sentence was taking place. All that day we milled around the compound, discussing the possibilities of our fate. That night when the interpreter came into the barracks, I asked if the men would be going to work the following day or if it was to be another "Japanese holiday."

By this time, we were thoroughly familiar with the Japanese calendar and could name all of the holidays. We knew that August held no days of commemoration.

The interpreter was reluctant to talk, but did volunteer the information that peace negotiations were underway, and that perhaps we would be going home soon. Even though we suspected as much, actually being told so by the Japs made us very happy. After breakfast the next morning, a committee of four of us went to the Japanese office, demanded to know more of the international situation, and were told the full details.

American planes had dropped a new deadly weapon on Hiroshima and Nagasaki which had killed most of the inhabitants of both cities; Japan, unable to combat the supernatural, had honorably surrendered to the Allied forces.

They informed us that Allied troops had not yet set foot on Japanese soil, but were expected to land soon.

Also, they said all aircraft we saw in the future would be that of the American Air Force. Promptly after our conference, we painted the letters "POW'" on the roof of our quarters as a signal to Allied aircraft and then proceeded to assume command of the camp.

We disarmed all of the guards, ordered the camp commander to vacate his quarters, and made it clear to the Japs that we expected them to exercise military courtesy when meeting or addressing any of us either in the camp or nearby village. When seeking those guards who had maltreated prisoners, we learned that they had departed on the preceding day and were not expected to return. In compliance with the Jap commander's request, we allowed him to keep his saber which was, he explained, a family heirloom handed down for generations. Returning our consideration, he promised to have a cow delivered on the hoof daily to the camp as long as we remained his guests. He also agreed to provide each man with ten cigarettes daily, and would contact Tokyo headquarters, inquiring just when American occupational troops were expected to land on the Japanese home islands. That night we enjoyed the sleep of free men; those of us who were not too excited to sleep!

The first morning after being informed that hostilities had ceased, we held our own roll call in place of the usual Japanese "Bango." When I commanded "Attention," instead of the familiar "ki wo tsuke," the men looked dazed. When "Right Dress" registered with them, instead of "migi noriai," it took several seconds for all to comprehend.

When time came for a count, and they heard instead of "Bango," the unfamiliar "Count off," nothing happened. I repeated the command, but to no avail, then in desperation I gave the command in Japanese. That did it. Down the ranks each man snapped his number, "ichi, ni, san, shi, go, roku, shichi, hachi, ku, ju, etc." (One, two, three, four, five, six, seven, eight, nine, ten, etc.) Shortly after breakfast that morning we heard the roar of planes and rushed outdoors to see them. There they were; a flight of nine Grumman shipboard fighters, flying directly over the camp at five thousand feet.

We couldn't definitely identify them until the leader of the flight obviously spotted our orange-painted "POW" on the roof and dived down to buzz the camp. On his tail came the entire flight, zooming over the treetops and dipping their wings as if to say, "Hi, boys. It's all over!"

On the morning of August 25, a B-29 flew low over the camp, dropping food supplies, candy, cigarettes, and clothing. This was our first view of the infamous "Bnijuku,"[18] and it was indeed impressive. We heard the roar of the ship before it came into view over the mountain top. When at last it did appear, we saw the nose of the ship first, and then the wings, and it seemed like minutes before the tail came into view. What a giant of the skies it was!

---

[18] Boeing B-29 Superfortress.

By noon we were all wearing American army clothing, including shoes, smoking Camels, and had our stomachs full of American food and candy.

Incidentally, I ate fifteen chocolate bars as fast as I could remove the wrappers, and then had a dinner consisting of canned meats, soups, and army rations. We sat up most of that night smoking and discussing future plans.

Thus, we lived for the following ten days, waiting for the arrival of occupational troops. During the days we roamed the village, many of the men fully armed with former Jap weapons; however, all of this armament was needless as the civilian populace seemed glad that hostilities had ceased and was more than friendly. They explained to us that leaflets dropped over Gifu from an American plane a few days previous to V-J Day had warned the residents of our valley to evacuate because it was the next community to be demolished.

By September 5, we had become justifiably impatient, and that night the American Captain assigned another sergeant and me to go to the village police station and arrange for our transportation out of the valley.

We spent the entire night in the police station arranging for a train to take us from the valley to the outside world. The Japs are great procrastinators and attempted to stall us as much as possible. They informed us that nothing could be arranged without the aid of a certain factory official, who had charge of transportation, whom we promptly ordered them to summon. We must have gotten the little fellow out of bed, for he looked rather bleary-eyed. He in turn informed us that he could do nothing without the presence of a certain railroad executive who had charge of trains on the main line. We dispatched a policeman on a bicycle to summon that man.

By 1 A.M. we had the entire party assembled in the police station, and over many cups of hot tea we made the necessary arrangements to leave the valley the following morning. My companion and I arrived back in camp at 6 A.M. with the good news for which everyone had been waiting. Word quickly spread in the valley that we were leaving, for when we arrived at the station that day, practically the entire community was on hand to see us off. We knew most of these simple people, and they had grown to like us. Before the train left, we exchanged goodbyes and many of the Japs were crying.

One mother with whom I had worked at the factory apologized for her husband's absence because he was ill, and he had asked her to say goodbye for him. She told me they were sorry to see us leave, but knew that we were going home to our loved ones and to the land of plenty. However, in a lowered voice she asked what would become of her and her family. I assured her that the American Red Cross would be on hand if starvation actually set in, and told her not to worry.

And there it was, the happiest day of my life; I was riding a flat car on the narrow-gauge railway en route to the coast to join the American forces. I was a free man with everything I ever dreamed of ahead of me.

Our guards, soldiers to the end, accompanied us on the trip. After three hours on the narrow-gauge, we arrived at the central station on the main railroad that would take us to the coast in twenty-four hours. When the train stopped, we ordered our Jap army escort to clear two coaches for our use. They complied with our command, explaining to the passengers that they would have to disembark and await a later train because we were American soldiers en route to join our forces.

They humbly bowed to us as they left the coaches. The train made several stops that afternoon, and at each station civilian Japs brought us buckets of hot water and towels. We had our own soap, which had been dropped to us by the B-29. Each time we finished washing, we left the remaining soap with the water carriers, knowing that where we were going there would be plenty of soap. These were a vanquished people, but not too proud to admit defeat. I admired their spirit.

As night fell, we found ourselves exhausted from the trip and all of the excitement of the day. As the lights were dimmed in the coaches, we soon fell asleep. About 2 A.M., I faintly recalled the train having stopped; then, as it began to move again, someone shook my shoulder and I looked up into the face of a smiling American.

He was a reporter for an American news syndicate, and had boarded the train at the last stop, Ise No Umi. He asked where my group had been interned, where we had been captured, etc.; then I proceeded to ask questions in rapid-fire succession.

"Was Japan's surrender unconditional in every respect?"

"Does Russia entertain any territorial ambitions in her occupation of Manchuria?"

"What is the name of our new president?"

"Is it true or Japanese propaganda that the men of Bataan and Corregidor are considered cowards in America for not having fought to the last man?"

"Were any American cities bombed or shelled by the Axis powers during the war?"

"Who is the heavyweight champion of the world?"

"What are the major league baseball standings?" and countless other questions which popped into my mind during the ensuing two hours.

At dawn that morning, the train stopped at a town called Arai Machi on the Southern Coast. When we saw a contingent of American Navy personnel walking shore patrol, we knew that we had reached our journey's end and promptly disembarked. A small body of Navy officers approached us, and the commander of the Jap guard unit which had accompanied us stepped forward to formally turn us over to our own forces. He was promptly pushed aside, and with the other members of his company placed under custody.

Unfortunately, as previously mentioned, the Japs responsible for the atrocities in our camp had fled shortly after V-J Day, but were later apprehended and tried as war criminals. Naval landing boats took us to the USS Rescue, which lay at anchor in the bay.

Once aboard the hospital ship, we were instructed to cast all of our clothing overboard, enter a hot shower and scrub with medicated soap. As we emerged from the shower room each man was sprayed with a disinfectant.

After being garbed in new navy uniforms, we were interviewed and examined by medical personnel. The sick men in our group were hospitalized on the ship and the remaining ones were sent to the nearby British destroyer, Wizard, for transport to Yokohama.

En route to Yokohama, we lounged on the deck of the destroyer and listened to a loudspeaker which played currently popular music, all of which, of course, was foreign to us.

When I heard Bing Crosby sing "I'm Dreaming of a White Christmas," I noticed that my cheeks were a little damp and blamed it on the spray of the ocean; but frankly, I was sitting with my back to the wind.

We arrived in Yokohama around midnight and spent the night on board the American troop transport USS Idaho. After our first American breakfast in nearly four years, we left via truck for Atsugi Airstrip outside of Tokyo.

It was there that I saw the first white women I had seen since 1941. They were stationed there with the Air Transport Command, working with communications and as hostesses aboard the planes. I felt disappointed in seeing them for they appeared to be hard and calloused, but I dismissed this from my mind by reasoning that they had been leading a strenuous life with the Army for a long period of time and could be expected to look dissipated.

We left Tokyo aboard a C-54 transport plane en route to Okinawa. Before leaving the Tokyo area, we circled Fujiyama and then flew down to Hiroshima and Nagasaki to view the destruction wrought by the atomic bomb.

It was dark when we landed on Okinawa, and once more we were a tired but very happy group of men.

The following morning after breakfast, one of my buddies entered my tent and introduced me to his brother, a Naval officer who was stationed on the island. It was a grand reunion for the two, and a lucky break for me, because the brother had a staff car at his disposal and took us on a tour of the island.

At the end of the ride, he took us to his quarters and invited us to write to our families. He dispatched the letters the following morning via air mail as "Official Business," and my parents heard from me on September 20, 1945; the first word of my liberation.

From Okinawa we were flown to Manila where I stayed for ten days. During that time, we were thoroughly examined, vaccinated and inoculated against practically everything, equipped with army clothing, and provided with the best in food and recreation. Nothing the Army had to offer was too good for us. Mess halls were open twenty-four hours daily, and the canteens offered us everything in their stock free of charge.

On the day I arrived in Manila, I was met by one of my former best friends in the States who was stationed with a replacement organization there. His duties were to provide for the welfare of repatriated prisoners; needless to say, he did everything in his power to make things comfortable for me in addition to telling me all of the news of my family and friends.

What a grand feeling it was to walk down the streets of Manila in the company of a loyal friend, knowing that once more I was completely free.

Later that evening, we visited one of the city's flourishing night clubs located on the seventh floor of a bombed hotel building. It seemed that the seventh floor was the only one wholly intact. It was there that I enjoyed the first floor show I had seen in years. One can imagine what a thrill it was to hear a seventeen-piece orchestra play, "You Belong to My Heart," in rhumba tempo to the accompaniment of a crooner.

During those ten days in Manila, I sought vainly for a glimpse of an American woman who didn't look hard, but finally reconciled myself to the fact that their use of cosmetics made them appear that way.

Naturally, long since, I have again become accustomed to their use and would think strangely of any woman who did not use them.

On October 25, 1945, I arrived in San Francisco on board a Coast Guard vessel, the USS Joseph Dyckman, and have been enjoying the courtesies of a free man ever since.

And just how does it feel to be free again?

To fully appreciate the sensation, one must be deprived of every little privilege and luxury of the American way of life for a period of years and then suddenly be cast back into that mode of living. My experience had been ghastly and wonderful all at the same time.

In exchange for the things I learned in those long years, I wouldn't accept a million dollars; but please, don't anyone offer me that same amount of money to re-live even one year of it!

THE END